Driven by Desire

The Path to Unstoppable Success

JW Radford

Dedication

To my wife, Mylika—my heart, my partner, and my greatest blessing. Thank you for your endless love, grace, and sacrifices, for standing beside me through every season, and for believing in this dream long before it became a reality. Your strength, patience, and unwavering faith in me made this book possible.

To my parents, Charles and Rhonda—for the foundation you built, the values you instilled, and the example you set. Your guidance shaped the person—and the author—I've become.

And to my children, Brion, Courtney, Cori, and Camille—my greatest inspiration. You are the reason I keep growing, keep learning, and keep dreaming bigger. This book exists because of you, and it's dedicated to you with all my love.

Acknowledgment

First and foremost, all glory, honor, and praise belong to God.

This book exists because of His grace, His guidance, and His unwavering presence in my life. Every success I have experienced, every lesson I have learned, and every obstacle I have overcome can be traced back to Him. Without God as my foundation, none of this would be possible.

There were moments when doubt was loud, when the journey felt heavy, and when the vision seemed distant. In those moments, God provided strength when mine ran out, clarity when I was uncertain, and peace when the path was unclear. He placed purpose in my heart long before I ever understood it and gave me the courage to pursue it step by step.

This work is not a testament to my ability, but to His faithfulness. If these pages inspire, motivate, or encourage even one person to rise higher, dream bigger, or walk more boldly in their purpose, it is only because God allowed it.

To Him be the credit for every opportunity, every door opened, every victory earned, and every lesson learned. I am simply a steward of what He has entrusted to me.

Thank You, God, for being the source, the sustainer, and the reason behind it all.

About the Author

Meet the indomitable JW Radford, visionary Founder of *Trust Consulting Services* and best-selling author.

His trailblazing work in motivational speaking and business consultancy has established him as a paragon of success. In a world filled with countless speakers and consultants, JW stands apart—a true testament to determination—building a $100 million enterprise from the ground up through his own effort and unwavering resolve.

JW's story is a tapestry woven with challenges and triumphs. As a devoted single father of four, he confronted uncertainty after an honorable departure from the military, forced by a formidable and incurable illness.

In the shadows of adversity, while battling depression and addiction, JW chose resilience over surrender. Every obstacle became a stepping stone, shaping his journey and allowing him to emerge as a beacon of hope. These experiences ignited a passion for resilience and endurance—powerful themes that resonate throughout his work. His ability to overcome hardship lies at the heart of his professional mission and continues to inspire all who strive for success against the odds.

Known for his infectious humor, JW delivers speeches filled with warmth and levity that balance the weight of his message. He has traveled the globe, inspiring audiences with his compelling call to hold fast to their dreams and to face every challenge with courage.

As a business consultant, JW boasts an outstanding record of guiding companies through turbulent times toward their goals. His skill in developing innovative strategies has earned him recognition as a trusted mentor who is wholly dedicated to the success of those he advises.

Through *Trust Consulting Services*, he remains a guiding light—empowering both businesses and individuals to overcome barriers and reach their full potential.

Beyond his role as a dynamic entrepreneur, captivating speaker, and prolific author, JW finds joy in travel, often alongside his wife, the equally accomplished author MJ Radford. Together, they explore new places and draw inspiration from the world's diversity. Yet his greatest fulfillment is found in the quiet moments with family.

His children—Brion, Courtney, Camille, and Cori—and his grandson, Nas, are the foundation of his life.

Surrounded by them, and with the enduring presence of his parents, JW is reminded that life's richest blessings are found in the bonds we nurture and the love we share, fueling his relentless drive and unwavering spirit.

Contents

Introduction

Welcome to the start of your own journey—messy, unpredictable, but yours all the same—of rediscovering and putting to work the raw, unstoppable force of passion.

Here's the thing: passion isn't some mystical force you either have or don't. It's a *habit*, built piece by piece in the choices you make every single day.

Let me tell you how I learned this the hard way.

It all started when I was stationed in Germany, serving my country, wearing my uniform with pride—while privately, my personal life was unraveling. I was going through a painful divorce, and I had four children who depended on me.

One day, after what I thought was just a shoulder injury from working out, I felt a strange tingling sensation down my left arm. I figured it was a pinched nerve or maybe a strained muscle. But when it didn't go away, I went to see the doctor. What I thought would be a quick diagnosis and some physical therapy turned into days of medical tests.

Then came the moment that changed everything. The doctor looked me in the eye and told me I had multiple sclerosis. He didn't sugarcoat it—he said it was incurable. He told me I would eventually end up in a wheelchair and likely lose the use of my other extremities.

At first, I didn't even know how to process it. But the military knew exactly what to do—they decided I was no longer fit for service. Just like that, my career was over. I was forced into medical retirement.

I was out of a job. Out of a career. Left with four children to raise on my own, staring down a future that seemed destined to trap me in a wheelchair. I was broken. And almost instantly, I fell into a deep depression. I withdrew from the world, shutting myself off from people who cared. My coping mechanism? Alcohol. It was the one thing that numbed the reality I didn't want to face.

Then one day… it just happened.

I was taking my kids to grab something to eat at Chipotle, one of their favorite places. On the way, I stopped at an ATM to withdraw twenty dollars. The screen flashed back at me: "Insufficient Funds."

That was the moment.

It was like lightning shot through my body and rebooted every circuit in my mind. The light came on, bright and blinding. My inner voice shouted, "What am I doing here? What happened to me? Oh, HELL NO! I have to get up! I'm not staying here. I have too much to do!"

That was the spark. That was the fire.

From that day forward, the passion inside me began to burn hotter with each sunrise. I had dreams too big to let my circumstances kill them. I told myself that I have to run, jump, and climb every day. I won't let this diagnosis define me. I am a fighter. I am a WARRIOR.

Maybe you've been in your career for decades. Maybe you're just starting out. Or maybe you're stuck in the middle, repeating the same routines and wondering why the fire's gone dim. Maybe, like me, life has knocked you down so hard you can't see a way back up.

Wherever you are, the ideas in this book are designed to help you notice what's been holding you back and show you how to turn small, deliberate shifts into a surge of momentum.

This book isn't here to hand you a pep talk you'll forget by next week; it's here to give you a framework, a set of tools, that will help you rediscover the energy, focus, and drive you thought you'd lost.

We'll dig into passion from every angle. Sometimes it'll be practical, sometimes a little funny, sometimes you'll probably think, *"Alright, that hit too close to home."* That's fine. This book is meant to help you walk away changed, not just briefly inspired.

So here's your starting point: reclaim your drive, put it back at the center, and let it shape how you work, how you lead, and how you live.

Don't expect perfection. *Expect progress.*

Once you see how to tap into passion with intention, you'll find yourself reaching levels of achievement that once felt out of reach, and doing it in a way that sticks.

"The greatest personal limitation is to be found not in the things you want to do and can't, but in the things you've never considered doing."

—Richard Bandler

Chapter 1: The Power of Passion

"Passion is the spark that lights the fire of purpose. Without purpose, passion burns out; with purpose, it becomes unstoppable."

—Robin Sharma

Passion is rocket fuel. It's what takes regular people—the kind who doubt themselves, who stumble, who start over—and pushes them into extraordinary territory.

You know the feeling: that electric buzz when you're all in, when the world falls away, and you're too absorbed to notice the clock. That's passion.

Calling it a 'drive' seems insufficient. It's so much more than that. It's the stubborn force that keeps you moving when the odds aren't in your favor.

Now imagine if you could hold onto that, so it doesn't just emerge in bursts, but as a steady current running through your life.

What doors would it open? What glass ceilings would it help you smash through?

Here's the truth: passion can flip a dream into reality, turn a vision into something solid, and transform a passing thought into a mission that outlasts you.

But let's not oversimplify. It's not only about feeling lit up inside. To be effective, passion needs to be harnessed, focused, and directed in ways that nudge you forward.

In this chapter, we'll dig into why passion isn't optional, but rather it is the very foundation of accomplishment and fulfillment.

Understanding Passion

Passion is not a passing thrill. It is a sustaining force, the current that runs beneath our choices and often dictates how far we are willing to go.

It pulls you forward in moments when inertia would otherwise keep you still. You sense it not in grand pronouncements but in the ordinary rhythms of life—the instinct to stay at your desk a little longer, the restless thought that wakes you at night, the conviction that something unfinished deserves more of you.

The question is not whether passion matters but why it proves decisive in shaping accomplishment.

At its foundation, passion is not as mysterious as it's been philosophized to be. It is an intensity rooted in "commitment," in the willingness to give yourself to a pursuit without assurance of reward.

It is visible in those who cannot speak of their work without their voices shifting, their expressions hardening with conviction, those who are resolute in their goals.

That level of engagement blurs the hours. It replaces routine with absorption.

Consider figures who have reshaped their fields, like Steve Jobs, who made use of the same passion.

At first glance, we might assume it was a technical achievement that drove Jobs. But in delving deeper, we find that he was thoroughly fixated on elegance, on a seamless integration of design and function.

He had a real passion for his works, not momentary enthusiasm, but an enduring refusal to settle, even when convention dictated otherwise.

That kind of commitment doesn't usually arrive fully formed. More often, passion takes shape gradually. It emerges through action, sometimes quietly, revealing itself only after you've spent enough time doing the work to realize you can't easily walk away.

In these moments, you discover that your effort has become disproportionate to any external demand. You continue because you are compelled to, not because you are told to.

Reflect for a moment on your own life. The work that gives you satisfaction often comes from small achievements: mastering a skill, finishing a task that challenged you, and making progress that felt uncertain the day before. They're often the first signals of something deeper stirring beneath the surface.

When you notice yourself returning to a pursuit again and again, not because you have to but because you want to, that's worth paying attention to. It suggests a shift from simple enjoyment to genuine engagement.

And here, the distinction matters.

Diversions can be pleasant, but they fade once the moment passes. Devotion, on the other hand, reshapes your priorities, rearranges your schedule, and refuses to be ignored. It's the difference between stopping at an idea and feeling compelled to bring that idea to life.

This is where achievement takes root. People who move beyond wishing and into doing aren't necessarily the most talented or the luckiest. What separates them is their willingness to pair ambition with staying power.

Some call this commitment "grit" or a blend of passion and perseverance that outpaces raw ability.

Passion without effort runs in circles. However, together they sustain momentum long enough to turn goals into reality. When passion directs effort, investment follows naturally.

Over time, hours accumulate not because they are assigned, but because they are *chosen,* i.e., you choose to spend time on the thing that gives you passion.

You will find a common trait among those who are passionate. Such individuals are persistent in the pursuit of knowledge, they refine their skills, and naturally gravitate toward others who share the same drive, trying to connect with like-minded individuals.

Over time, these connections form more than just networks; they become "communities" built around shared energy and purpose.

Passion does not stay contained—that is not one of its characteristics. Instead, it multiplies, spreading through collaboration and mutual encouragement. From there, the influence grows outward.

When people see genuine commitment, they don't need to be pushed; they're drawn in. That is why passion is considered a necessary force for leaders.

A leader whose passion is visible doesn't coerce; they set an example that others want to match. In this sense, passion itself becomes a form of leadership.

In the workplace, it shows up as innovation: the urge to test new approaches even when the old ones "work well enough."

For entrepreneurs, it becomes a determination to keep building despite limited resources.

In relationships, passion steadies bonds by keeping both partners invested not only in each other but in the pursuit of shared goals that stretch beyond the individual.

It's also worth noting that passion is not fixed. What engages you at twenty may not be what sustains you later in life. That shift doesn't mean passion has vanished; it means it has evolved.

The key is to remain open, adjusting while staying true to the core of what energizes you most.

Of course, passion is not invulnerable. Criticism, setbacks, and fatigue can dull it. Yet those same moments reveal its deeper resilience. Passion allows you to pause, reassess, and return with renewed purpose.

The obstacles most of us fear—failure, judgment, even the pressure of success—are real. But passion changes the weight of those fears. It closes the distance between hesitation and action, making inaction harder to bear than risk.

That is why passion cannot be treated as optional. It separates those who simply persist from those who create.

Discovering and committing to your passion means taking responsibility for shaping the course of your own life.

So ask yourself: what work makes time disappear? What leaves you with more energy at the end than when you began?

The answer is none other than the 'passions' for which you are best geared.

Following them will allow you to propel yourself at work, in relationships, and in contributions that carry weight.

Recognizing your true passion is certainly the first step, but acting on it will turn the improbable into the achievable and the natural next step forward.

Why Passion Fuels Success

Imagine waking up not with the weight of another long day, but with an urgency you can't ignore, the pull to get started, to move toward something that matters.

People who have tapped into real passion do so routinely. For them, passion is not some fleeting high that comes from time to time, in random, incoherent bursts; it is a steady current, a force that transforms ordinary effort into extraordinary achievement.

Think of passion as the ignition switch. Without it, even the most capable engine sits idle. With it, work stops feeling like a grind and starts to *flow*.

Why does passion have this kind of power?

For one, people who are passionate go further. They give more of themselves, not reluctantly, but willingly.

And when difficulties pile up—as they always do—passion keeps them pressing forward. Where others stop, they continue.

This is the difference between intent and achievement: the willingness to keep moving when the outcome isn't guaranteed.

That persistence also builds resilience in the individual, allowing him to not be deterred by setbacks.

To him or her, a setback never ends the story; it becomes another part of the process.

If you've ever been deeply invested in a project, you know this: rejection stings, failure hurts, but passion keeps you in the game. It shortens the time between falling and standing up again. And once you've gotten back up, you never fail to begin.

Yet resilience by itself is not enough. Passion deepens when paired with deliberate practice, the kind where individuals return repeatedly to their work, push just beyond their current ability, and refine their skills over time. Again, the effort you make to get back into the game is vital here.

It is this structure, not just enthusiasm, that transforms raw effort into mastery. Passion makes the discipline tolerable, even desirable.

Still, the most enduring passion does more than sharpen skills. It aligns with *purpose*. People who sustain their passion often connect it to something larger than themselves: solving a problem, advancing a cause, or creating value for others.

Without that alignment, enthusiasm drifts. With it, passion acquires depth and longevity, giving people the drive they desire to continue moving without fail.

This also explains why passion outperforms external rewards. While money, status, or recognition can spark short bursts of motivation, they rarely sustain it.

Passion, on the other hand, becomes the internal engine that keeps turning long after the applause has faded. It is the link that connects autonomy, mastery, and purpose—the three pillars of lasting motivation.

Passion fuels the drive to work without being forced, to return to the task again and again, and to stretch just beyond current ability. It also ties effort to meaning, reminding you that the hours invested are not just about outcomes but about building something that matters.

In this way, passion doesn't compete with external rewards—it renders them secondary, because the satisfaction of the work itself becomes the most compelling reward. In doing so, it shifts energy away from short-term incentives toward long-term meaning.

With that momentum comes focus. When you care deeply about something, you naturally tune out distractions. Attention sharpens. Decisions become simpler because passion clarifies what aligns and what doesn't. Saying "no" gets easier when you have a clear "yes" guiding you forward. That kind of focus is what turns scattered effort into consistent progress.

And consistent progress brings us to talent. Talent alone, as we know, is rarely decisive. There are countless gifted individuals who never fully realize their potential.

The real difference lies in sustained effort, fueled by passion. Passion bridges the gap between what you're capable of and what you consistently practice. It turns skill into mastery, good work into excellent work, and persistence into a breakthrough.

Think about the names that come up when we talk about innovation—Jobs, Musk, Winfrey. Talent played a role, of course, but what stands out is how deeply passion infused everything they touched.

They weren't content to operate within boundaries. They expanded them because they were too invested not to.

There's another element worth underscoring: authenticity. Passion makes you genuine. When you care deeply, there's no need for pretense. Others can see it. They trust it.

In a world where so much feels manufactured, authenticity becomes its own kind of currency. It builds relationships that endure, partnerships that grow, and doors that open when credentials alone might not.

And unlike physical energy, passion renews itself. It can fade, but it can also be rekindled through new challenges, fresh perspectives, or simply returning to the core of why you started.

People who remain passionate over time do not do so naturally; it is because they choose to evolve with it.

Perhaps most overlooked: passion adds joy.

Not surface-level excitement, but a deep satisfaction. Success, when driven by passion, isn't only about crossing a finish line; it's about valuing the miles along the way. Arguably, this is one of the most compelling reasons for individuals to stick with their work as they find real joy in it.

This is why passion is so often called the lifeblood of success. It doesn't just drive innovation or fuel perseverance; it makes the journey itself meaningful.

Without passion, progress feels like an obligation.

With it, the same path feels like discovery.

So pause and ask yourself: Where does time disappear for you? What pursuits leave you more alive at the end than at the beginning?

Those are not trivial questions. They are the signals of work that will compound, endure, and give meaning to setbacks.

To follow them is to transform what once seemed improbable into the natural next step forward.

Chapter 2: Discovering Your Inner Fire

"The cave you fear to enter holds the treasure you seek."

—Joseph Campbell

That ATM moment I told you about? It wasn't magic. It wasn't some mystical awakening where the universe suddenly handed me all the answers.

What happened was this: I finally stopped running from who I really was.

See, for months after my diagnosis, I'd been trying to be the version of myself that everyone expected. The stoic veteran who takes everything in stride. The father who has it all figured out. The man who doesn't break down when life throws him a curveball.

But standing there with "Insufficient Funds" staring back at me, I realized I'd been living someone else's story. And that story was killing me.

This chapter is about returning to your true self, not the version you've been told to become, but the one that has always been there. The self with unruly dreams that don't always fit into tidy boxes. The self whose passions may seem puzzling to others yet continue to glow inside you all the same.

What I've come to realize is this: your spark isn't buried in some unreachable place. It's close, waiting for the moment you choose to notice it instead of pushing it aside.

Identifying Your True Desires

Let me ask you something: When was the last time you wanted something so badly that it kept you awake at night? Not worried awake… excited awake. The kind where your mind races with possibilities instead of problems.

If you can't remember, don't worry. That fire is still there. It's just been buried under layers of what other people told you to want.

Start here: grab a pen and paper. I'm serious… not your phone, not your laptop. Something physical. Write down the last time you felt genuinely excited about anything. Could be work, could be a hobby, could be something you saw someone else doing that made you think, "I wish I could do that."

Don't edit yourself. Don't worry if it sounds ridiculous. Just write.

I'll give you an example from my own life. During my lowest season, sinking into depression and staring at an empty bank account, there was still one thing that gave me a sense of life: helping others work through their problems.

It didn't matter whether a neighbor needed guidance with their business or one of my kids was stuck on homework. Each time, something inside me came alive when I could untangle the mess and show a path forward. That's how *Trust Consulting Services* was born, not from some grand business plan, but from recognizing what made me come alive even when everything else felt dead.

Your desires are like that, too. They're the activities that make time disappear. The conversations that energize you instead of drain you. The problems you actually enjoy solving.

But here's where most people get stuck: they confuse what they think they should want with what they actually want.

Society has this script for us, right? Get a steady job, climb the corporate ladder, buy the house, get the car, retire at 65. And for some people, that script works. But for others, maybe for you, that script feels like a prison sentence.

I spent my early career following someone else's script. Good soldier, follow orders, don't rock the boat. And you know what? I was miserable. I was successful by conventional standards, but I was dying inside.

It wasn't until I had no choice, when MS forced me out of that script, that I discovered what I actually wanted: to build something of my own, to help people on my own terms, to create value in ways that felt authentic to me.

So let me ask you again: What do you actually want? Not what you think you should want. Not what would impress your parents, your friends, or your LinkedIn connections. What makes you come alive?

Sometimes the answer surprises you. Maybe you're an accountant who dreams of teaching. Maybe you're a teacher who wants to start a business. Maybe you're a successful executive who secretly wants to write novels.

Here's what I learned: your true desires don't have to make sense to anyone else. They just have to be true to you.

And if you're thinking, "But I can't just abandon everything to chase some dream," I get it. I had four kids to feed and bills to pay. You don't have to blow up your life overnight.

Start small. Give yourself permission to experiment. Always wanted to write? Start a blog. Interested in photography? Take a weekend class. Curious about starting a business? Begin with a side project.

The key is to start moving toward what excites you instead of just away from what you don't like.

I also want to address something that trips up a lot of people: the difference between ego desires and authentic desires.

Ego desires are the ones that sound impressive. "I want to be CEO." "I want to make a million dollars." "I want to be famous."

Nothing wrong with those goals, but ask yourself why you want them. If it's because you think they'll prove something to other people, that's ego talking.

Authentic desires feel different. They're quieter, more personal. They're about contribution, connection, and creation. They're about becoming who you're meant to be, not proving who you think you should be.

When I was building my business, there were plenty of times I could have taken shortcuts or made decisions based on what would look good on paper. But the desires that kept me going: helping people, creating something meaningful, proving to myself and my kids that setbacks don't have to be permanent; those were authentic.

And here's the thing about authentic desires: they have staying power. When the going gets tough (and it will), authentic desires keep you moving. Ego desires tend to evaporate under pressure.

So spend some time with this. Write down what excites you. Pay attention to what energizes you versus what drains you. Notice what you're naturally curious about.

And don't worry if it takes time to figure out. I'm still discovering new aspects of what drives me, and I'm in my fifties. This isn't a one-time exercise; it's an ongoing conversation with yourself.

The goal isn't to have all the answers immediately. The goal is to start listening to the part of you that knows what you really want, even if it's been quiet for a while.

Embracing Your Authentic Self

Here's a hard truth I learned the expensive way: pretending to be someone else is exhausting.

For years, before my diagnosis, during my military career, even in the early days of my business, I spent so much energy trying to be who I thought I was supposed to be that I barely had any left for actually being myself.

Even in my marriage, I found myself living a lie. Looking back now, I can admit without hesitation: I was in a bad marriage. That's a story big enough to demand its own book, but for this moment, I'll just say that somewhere along the way, I stopped being a husband and started being an actor.

I knew I didn't love my children's mother. Truthfully, I barely even liked her. But I convinced myself that love wasn't required—that the role I played was enough. So I put on the mask every morning and every evening. I smiled at family gatherings. I held her hand in public. I played the part of the faithful husband for my children, for the church pews that were always watching, for friends and family who thought they knew our story.

The performance didn't stop there; it became my way of life. While serving in the military, I decided to take on a part-time job just to keep myself out of the house. I would leave at six in the morning and sometimes not return until one a.m. And still, before I even stepped inside, I'd sit in the driveway for ten long minutes, gripping the steering wheel, whispering prayers. Praying that she would already be asleep. Praying that God, or anyone, would give me the strength to walk through the door with a smile. Because no matter how much I wanted to collapse from exhaustion or let the truth show on my face, my children were always waiting. And when those little faces lit up, "Daddy's home!" I never wanted to ruin that moment for them.

Behind closed doors, though, the weight of that performance crushed me. It wasn't just unfair to her—it was unfair to my kids, who deserved to see what real love looked like, not a staged version. And it was especially unfair to me. I was slowly suffocating under the weight of a life I didn't want, rehearsing lines for a play I no longer believed in.

That's the thing about faking it to make it: at first, it feels like survival. You tell yourself you're doing the noble thing, the selfless thing. But over time, the pretense rots you from the inside out. Faking confidence is one thing. Faking joy might even get you through a hard season. But faking love—faking life itself—comes with a cost you can't outrun. Eventually, the truth rises to the surface, demanding to be acknowledged. And when it does, you realize that pretending isn't protecting anyone—it's only prolonging the inevitable.

The military taught me to be disciplined, stoic, and unflappable. Great qualities, but taken to an extreme, they became a prison. When I got my MS diagnosis, I thought I had to handle it like a perfect soldier—no fear, no doubt, no vulnerability.

That performance nearly destroyed me.

It wasn't until I hit rock bottom, sitting in that Chipotle parking lot, staring at an ATM screen that basically told me I was broke, that I finally stopped pretending. In that moment, all the masks fell away. I wasn't a veteran or a father or anything else. I was just a scared, angry human being who had run out of ways to pretend everything was okay.

And you know what? That moment of brutal honesty is what saved me.

Because when you stop trying to be who you think you should be, you can finally start becoming who you actually are.

Authenticity isn't about perfection. It's about truth. It's about acknowledging that you're flawed, complicated, and still figuring things out, and that's okay. In fact, that's what makes you human.

The business world loves to talk about "authentic leadership" and "being genuine," but most of the time, what they really mean is "be authentic in a way that's comfortable for everyone else." That's not authenticity, that's performance with better marketing.

Real authenticity is messy. It means admitting when you don't know something. It means being vulnerable about your struggles. It means making decisions based on your values, even when they're not popular.

When I started sharing my story about the MS diagnosis, the depression, and the financial struggles, people told me I was crazy. "You don't tell potential clients that you were suicidal," they said. "You don't admit weakness in business."

But here's what happened: the more honest I was about my journey, the more people connected with me. Not despite my struggles, but because of them. Because everyone is fighting battles they don't talk about, and when someone is brave enough to go first, it gives others permission to be human, too.

That vulnerability became the foundation of everything I built. My business grew not because I pretended to have all the answers, but because I was honest about the questions I was still figuring out.

Now, I'm not saying you should overshare in every situation. Professional boundaries exist for good reasons. But there's a difference between being professional and being fake.

Authenticity in professional settings might look like admitting when you're wrong, asking for help when you need it, or making decisions that align with your values even when they're difficult.

In personal relationships, it might mean having conversations you've been avoiding, setting boundaries that protect your energy, or finally pursuing interests you've been putting off because they don't fit other people's expectations of who you are.

The science backs this up, by the way. Research shows that people who live authentically, meaning their actions align with their values and beliefs, report higher levels of life satisfaction, better relationships, and even better physical health.

When you're constantly performing, your stress hormones stay elevated. When you can relax into being yourself, your body and mind can finally relax too.

But let's be real: authenticity takes courage. When you stop people-pleasing and start being honest about who you are, some people won't like it. They'll miss the version of you that always said yes, that never caused problems, that made them comfortable.

That's their loss, not yours.

The people who matter, the ones who will stick with you through the real challenges of life, want to know the real you anyway. The rest were never really in your corner to begin with.

I think about this a lot when I'm mentoring other entrepreneurs. So many of them are exhausted from trying to be the person they think investors want to see, or customers want to buy from, or employees want to work for.

But the most successful people I know, the ones who build businesses that last, who have relationships that sustain them, who wake up excited about their lives, they're all just being themselves, at a higher volume.

They've figured out how to take who they authentically are and amplify the best parts of it.

That's what I want for you. Not to become someone different, but to become more fully yourself.

Start by paying attention to the moments when you feel most alive, most energized, most like yourself. What's different about those moments? Who are you with? What are you doing?

Then ask yourself: how can I create more moments like that?

It might mean changing jobs, or it might just mean changing how you approach your current job. It might mean having difficult conversations with people you love, or it might mean finally signing up for that class you've been thinking about.

The point is to start moving in the direction of authenticity, even if you can only take small steps at first.

Because here's what I know for sure: the world doesn't need another perfect person. It needs more people who are brave enough to be real.

Your authentic self, with all your flaws, fears, and contradictions, has something to offer that no one else can. But only if you're willing to stop hiding it.

So take off the mask. Stop performing. Start being.

The fire you're looking for is already there. It's been waiting for you to stop pretending it doesn't exist.

Chapter 3: The Science Behind Passion

"The brain is wider than the sky."

—Emily Dickinson

I'll be straight with you: I don't have a science degree.

No Ph.D hanging on my wall, no lab coat in my closet. What do I have? An obsession with figuring out why some people keep pushing when everything says stop.

I've read stacks of books on this… not dense academic texts, but accessible stuff written for regular people trying to understand what makes motivation tick. And here's what surprised me: passion has biology behind it. Real, measurable brain activity that you can actually track.

This chapter won't turn you into a neuroscientist. But knowing even a little about what's happening upstairs when passion kicks in? That changes how you treat it. You stop sitting around waiting to feel motivated and start building the conditions that make motivation show up more often.

Because passion isn't magic, it's mechanics. And once you see the mechanics, you can work with them.

Neuroscience and Passion

Your brain runs on chemistry. Sounds clinical, but it's actually pretty straightforward once you break it down.

There's this neurotransmitter called dopamine. It floods your system when something feels rewarding… finishing a tough project, nailing a presentation, doing work that actually matters. People call dopamine the "feel-good" chemical, but that's not quite right. It's more accurate to call it the 'do-that-again' chemical.

Here's the basic sequence: A region called the ventral tegmental area releases dopamine. That dopamine travels to your nucleus accumbens, essentially your pleasure hub. Then your prefrontal cortex, which handles planning and decisions, evaluates whether whatever you just did is worth repeating.

Think of it like a relay. One part starts, another receives, a third evaluates. When you're genuinely passionate about something, that whole circuit reinforces itself. You do the thing, get the dopamine hit, want to do it again. Loop complete.

But dopamine's got company. Serotonin regulates mood and creates contentment. Oxytocin strengthens bonds and builds trust, which explains why passionate groups feel so energized. When these chemicals work together, they create something bigger than each one alone. That's the neurological reality of passion: multiple systems firing in coordination.

Your amygdala, the part that processes emotional responses, also gets involved. When you're passionate, your amygdala heightens emotional engagement, stamping certain experiences as significant. That's why you remember passion-related moments with unusual clarity. Your brain literally marked them as important.

Now here's where it gets practical: neuroplasticity. Your brain rewires itself based on what you repeatedly do and think. When you consistently work on something you care about, you're forming new neural pathways and strengthening existing connections. You're making it physically easier for your brain to access skills and knowledge related to your passion.

Learning any skill demonstrates this. Early on, it requires conscious effort. After consistent practice, it becomes automatic. That's not just a habit; it's changing your brain's architecture.

Passion also affects stress in tangible ways. When you're genuinely engaged in meaningful work, your brain releases endorphins. These natural chemicals don't just mask discomfort; they reduce mental strain. That's why someone can work twelve hours on a passion project without the same exhaustion that six hours at a hated job creates. The endorphins buffer against fatigue.

But these same mechanisms can work against you. Push too hard for too long, and your prefrontal cortex gets overwhelmed by the constant chemical flood. Like any system, it can overload. The engine that powers you can stall if you don't manage it properly.

Managing it means setting milestones that provide regular wins without demanding constant maximum intensity. It means building rest periods where your brain consolidates learning and recharges. Mindfulness practices help here; they train your brain to modulate its own responses instead of getting hijacked by every spike of passion or stress.

There's also research on mirror neurons worth knowing about. These fire both when you perform an action and when you watch someone else do it. Reading about someone achieving what you're working toward? Your mirror neurons fire as if you were doing it. That vicarious experience reinforces your passion and demonstrates the possibility to your brain.

This explains why community matters for sustaining passion. Around other passionate people, your mirror neurons constantly activate. Their energy literally transfers through this neural mechanism.

One more piece: passionate activities stimulate neurogenesis; new neuron formation, especially in your hippocampus, which handles memory and learning. Pursuing your passion doesn't just feel satisfying; it's expanding your brain's capacity to learn and remember. Passion makes learning easier, and learning deepens passion. Self-reinforcing cycle.

Bottom line: when you engage deeply with something you genuinely care about, you're not just having a good time. You're activating multiple brain systems that boost performance, build resilience, and physically restructure your neural architecture to support your goals.

Understanding this doesn't make the work easier. But it makes sense. When you know the struggle comes with real, beneficial brain changes, trusting the process gets simpler.

Psychological Impact of Determined Desire

There's a particular energy that comes with genuinely wanting something. Not surface-level interest. Not temporary excitement. Something deeper that doesn't let go even when circumstances push back.

Psychologically, this creates what researchers call cognitive persistence. Your brain keeps working on passion-related problems even when you're not actively thinking about them. You're doing something completely unrelated, and suddenly... solution.

This happens because when you deeply want something, your brain treats it as a priority. It allocates processing power to it, even in the background. During sleep, during routine tasks, and during moments when your conscious attention is elsewhere, your brain keeps working on the problem.

Like a program running in the background on your computer. You don't see it actively working, but it's processing, connecting, finding patterns.

This creates an attention filter. When you care intensely about something, you naturally notice related opportunities and information you'd otherwise miss. Psychologists call this your Reticular Activating System, your brain's filter that highlights what's relevant to your goals. But it only works effectively with a genuine desire driving it.

Without that desire, the filter stays wide open, letting in everything and nothing. With it, the filter becomes precisely tuned.

Now let's talk resilience. This is where determined desire proves its value.

When you want something intensely, setbacks become data points instead of endpoints. Rejection isn't personal judgment; it's information about what to try differently. This connects to what psychologists call "grit," passion plus perseverance, predicting success better than talent or intelligence.

But here's the key: determination only works long-term when passion powers it. Determination alone is just stubbornness. It creates burnout because you're forcing yourself forward without internal fuel. It is powered by genuine desire, which sustains itself because every push forward connects to why you're doing it.

There's also a social dimension. When you have determined desire, people sense it. Authentic passion attracts, not in a manipulative way, but in a way that makes others want to support you. Opportunities often arise not from credentials but because someone saw genuine commitment and wanted involvement.

But there's a shadow side worth addressing. Determined desire can become problematic without self-awareness.

When you want something that intensely, you risk becoming so single-minded that relationships suffer, health deteriorates, or perspective disappears.

The solution isn't dampening desire; it's expanding awareness around it. Regularly asking: Is this desire serving my whole life, or has it become a tyrant demanding everything else be sacrificed?

Psychologically healthy desire integrates with your values rather than conflicting with them. It enhances life rather than consuming it.

There's also the question of authentic versus borrowed desire. Sometimes what feels like determined desire is actually someone else's dream you've internalized. You think you desperately want something because that's what success looks like in your context, when what you actually want is completely different.

Simple test: Does pursuing this energize or deplete you? Real desire, even when work is hard, leaves you feeling more alive. Borrowed desire, regardless of achievement level, leaves you feeling empty.

Determined desire also transforms your relationship with time. When you deeply want something, time becomes an ally instead of an enemy. You stop feeling like you're running out and start seeing each day as another opportunity to move toward your goal.

This shift matters. Instead of time pressure creating anxiety, it creates urgency and positive motivation to maximize available time.

Another benefit: determined desire creates decision-making clarity. When you're clear about what you want, choices simplify. Saying no to misaligned things and yes to aligned things gets easier. This clarity filters your thoughts, too. It lets in productive thinking while blocking noise and distraction. When you know what you want with certainty, doubt has less operating room.

But that intensity requires management. The psychological fire of determined desire needs tending. It needs rest, balance, reflection, perspective, and self-care sustainability.

Think of desire like a flame. Too small provides insufficient light or warmth. Too large and uncontained, it burns everything around it. The goal is to maintain the right intensity, strong enough to guide and motivate, and controlled enough to sustain.

Your desire doesn't have to start fully formed. It often builds over time, strengthened by small wins and deepened by obstacles overcome. However, once you find something worth having a determined desire for and fully commit to it, the psychological transformation is substantial.

You become someone who doesn't just want success; you become someone psychologically structured to achieve it. Your attention, decisions, resilience, relationships—everything aligns around what you genuinely desire.

That's the real power of determined desire. It doesn't just change what you do. It changes who you are.

Chapter 4: Setting Long-Term Goals

"A goal without a plan is just a wish."

—Antoine de Saint-Exupéry

Here's what I've learned about goals: everyone has them, but most people treat them like New Year's resolutions, exciting for about three weeks, then forgotten by February.

The difference between goals that fade and goals that actually happen? A real plan. Not a vague intention or a hopeful thought, but an actual map showing how you get from where you are to where you want to be.

After my ATM moment, I had plenty of motivation. What I didn't have was a clue about how to turn that motivation into something tangible. I wanted to build a business, support my kids, and prove that my diagnosis wasn't the final word on my life. Great. But wanting isn't having, and wishing isn't working.

So I had to figure out how to take this fire inside me and channel it into something concrete. That meant getting specific about what I actually wanted and building a step-by-step process to get there.

This chapter is about doing that work. Not the sexy part of chasing dreams, but the necessary part: the planning, the structure, the deliberate choices that turn possibility into reality.

Let me tell you about the first real business plan I ever wrote.

It was terrible. Pages of buzzwords and optimistic projections with basically no connection to reality. I showed it to a mentor, expecting praise. Instead, he looked at me and said, "This doesn't tell me what you're actually going to do. It tells me what you hope might happen. Those aren't the same thing."

That stung. But he was right.

Vision isn't daydreaming. It's creating a specific, detailed picture of what you're building and why it matters. When your vision is clear, decisions become simpler. You know what fits and what doesn't.

Here's how I think about it: vision answers the "what" and the "why." What are you building? Why does it matter? Not just to the world, but to you specifically. What's the point of this effort?

For me, the vision started simple: build a consulting business that helps other businesses solve complex problems. But that's still pretty vague, right? Lots of people consult. What made mine different?

I had to dig deeper. Why consulting? Because I'm good at seeing patterns others miss and finding solutions to messy problems. Why businesses specifically? Because that's where I could have the most impact and generate the income I needed. Why did it matter? Because I needed to prove to myself and my kids that setbacks don't define you.

That's vision. Specific enough to guide decisions, meaningful enough to sustain effort.

But vision alone doesn't cut it. You need clarity, too.

Clarity takes your vision and breaks it into components you can actually work with. It's the difference between "I want to be successful" and "I want to generate $500,000 in revenue by serving mid-sized manufacturing companies facing supply chain challenges."

See the difference? One sounds nice. The other gives you something to aim at.

Getting to clarity requires honest reflection. You've got to strip away what you think you should want and figure out what you actually want. That means ignoring the noise, other people's expectations, societal scripts about success, and all the 'shoulds' that have piled up over the years.

Sit with yourself. Really sit. What matters to you? Not what sounds impressive, but what genuinely pulls you forward?

Here's a practical approach: write down your vision, then ask "what does that actually mean?" five times. Each answer gets more specific, more real.

Example:

- I want to be successful.

- What does that mean? I want financial security and professional respect.

- What does that mean? I want to earn enough to provide for my family while doing work that challenges me.

- What does that mean? I want to generate $X in revenue serving clients who value strategic thinking.

- What does that mean? I need to land Y clients paying Z for services A, B, and C.

- What does that mean? I need to develop expertise in specific areas, build a referral network, and create a service delivery system.

Now you've got something workable.

Vision and clarity also need regular maintenance. Your first clear vision won't be your last. As you grow, as circumstances change, your vision should evolve too. That's not failure… that's adaptation.

I revisit my vision quarterly. Sometimes nothing changes. Sometimes I realize I'm chasing something that doesn't matter anymore and need to redirect. Both outcomes are valuable.

One more thing: vision needs to be yours. Not borrowed from someone else's playbook. Not copied from whoever you admire. Yours.

When I started, I tried modeling my business after other consultants I respected. That was fine for learning mechanics, but their vision wasn't mine. Their "why" wasn't my "why."

Once I stopped trying to be them and focused on being the best version of me, things clicked.

Your vision should energize you, not drain you. If thinking about your goals feels like an obligation rather than an opportunity, something's off. Either the goal isn't really yours, or you haven't connected it to what genuinely matters to you.

Clarity also means knowing what you're not doing. Every yes to one thing is a no to something else. Being clear about your vision helps you say no to opportunities that look good on paper but don't serve your actual goals.

I've turned down projects that would have paid well because they didn't align with where I was building. Early on, that was hard. Money was tight. But staying focused on the vision meant protecting my limited time and energy for things that actually moved me forward.

Here's the practical reality: vision and clarity aren't mystical. They're the result of thinking deeply about what you want, being honest about why you want it, and getting specific about what success actually looks like.

Do that work. Write it down. Revisit it regularly. Let it evolve as you do.

Because without a clear vision, you're just wandering. And wandering might be fine for a hike, but it's no way to build a life.

Creating a Roadmap to Success

Having vision is crucial. But vision without a plan is just sophisticated wishing.

I learned this the expensive way. I knew what I wanted: a successful consulting business, financial stability, and proof that I could build something significant despite my circumstances. Great vision. Zero roadmap.

So I started working. Hard. Really hard. Eighty-hour weeks. Taking any client who'd pay. Saying yes to everything. And you know what happened? I was busy, exhausted, and not actually moving forward. I was working hard but not working smart.

That's when I realized that effort without direction is just motion. You need a map showing how Point A connects to Point B, with all the steps in between.

Here's how to build that map.

Start with your destination. Not vague… specific. For me, it was hitting a certain revenue number while serving a specific type of client in a way that let me be present for my kids. Your destination will be different. Define it precisely.

Next, work backward. If that's where you want to be in five years, where do you need to be in three years? In one year? In six months? This creates waypoints, intermediate goals that mark real progress.

These waypoints matter. They break an overwhelming long-term goal into manageable chunks. Instead of "build a million-dollar business," it's "land three anchor clients this quarter." Way less intimidating, way more actionable.

Now here's where most people stop. They've got their waypoints marked. They think that's enough. It's not.

Each waypoint needs its own action plan. What specific steps get you from where you are now to that next waypoint? Break those down into monthly actions, then weekly tasks, then daily habits.

For example, if your quarterly goal is landing three anchor clients, your monthly action might be having twenty qualified conversations. Your weekly task might be reaching out to ten prospects. Your daily habit might be spending an hour on outreach and relationship building.

See how that works? You've taken "build a business" and turned it into "spend an hour today doing this specific thing." That's the power of a real roadmap.

But roadmaps need flexibility built in. Life doesn't follow scripts. You'll hit detours, dead ends, and unexpected opportunities. A rigid plan breaks under pressure. A flexible roadmap adapts.

I planned to grow through direct outreach. What actually worked? Referrals from existing clients. My roadmap shifted to focus on client satisfaction and relationship depth instead of volume prospecting. Same destination, different route.

That's fine. Expected, even. The point isn't following the map perfectly; it's having a map to adjust when reality hits.

Time management becomes critical here. You've got a roadmap, great. But if you're not protecting time to actually follow it, nothing happens. This means getting ruthless about priorities.

I started tracking my time for two weeks. Eye-opening. Hours vanished into reactive tasks that felt urgent but didn't move anything forward. Once I saw that pattern, I could fix it, blocking time for high-impact work, batching similar tasks, and eliminating time drains.

Use whatever system works for you. Calendars, to-do lists, project management apps, whatever. The tool matters less than the commitment to use it consistently.

Accountability helps enormously. Tell someone your roadmap. Regular check-ins create external pressure to follow through. I meet with a small group of other business owners monthly. We review progress, share obstacles, and push each other forward. That external accountability makes a real difference.

Also, build in regular review periods. Monthly minimum, quarterly better. Look at your roadmap honestly. Are you making progress? Why or why not? What needs adjustment?

These reviews aren't about beating yourself up when things don't go perfectly. They're about learning and adapting. What worked this month? Do more of that. What didn't? Figure out why and try something different.

And here's something people forget: celebrate progress. Not just big wins, but small ones too. Hit your weekly target?

Acknowledge it. Reached a waypoint? Mark it somehow. These celebrations matter. They reinforce the behaviors that got you there and keep motivation high when the full journey still stretches ahead.

Your roadmap should also account for learning. You don't know everything you'll need to know when you start. Build in time for skill development, knowledge acquisition, and seeking guidance from people further along the path.

I blocked time for reading, for courses, for conversations with people doing what I wanted to do. That wasn't wasted time; it was essential to reaching my destination because I needed capabilities I didn't have yet.

One more critical piece: your roadmap needs to align with your values. If the path you've charted requires sacrificing things that matter to you, you'll either abandon the roadmap or damage yourself following it.

Figure out your non-negotiables and build them into the plan.

Here's the bottom line: a roadmap turns 'someday' into "this week." It converts hope into action. It gives you something concrete to work on today that moves you toward where you want to be tomorrow.

Without it, you're hoping luck and effort align. With it, you're systematically building the life you decided you want.

Take the time to build your roadmap properly. Make it detailed but flexible. Review and adjust it regularly. Protect time to actually follow it. Celebrate progress along the way.

And remember: the roadmap isn't the destination. It's the tool that helps you get there. Don't confuse having a plan with doing the work. The plan matters, but execution matters more.

So build your roadmap. Then follow it. Adjust it when needed. Keep moving forward.

That's how vision becomes reality.

Chapter 5: Overcoming Obstacles

"The gem cannot be polished without friction, nor man perfected without trials."

—Chinese Proverb

Let me tell you something about going after what matters to you: obstacles aren't just occasional visitors that drop by now and then. They're more like roommates who never leave.

You'd think that once you nail down your vision and map out your plan, everything would fall into place. I wish it worked that way. Truth is, challenges keep showing up, and each one basically asks you the same question: Do you really want this or not?

Here's what separates those who make it from those who don't. It's not about avoiding problems but what happens when you hit them.

Some folks run into their first real wall and think the universe is telling them to quit. Others? They expect walls. They know they're coming, so they just figure out how to climb over, go around, or bust through. One barrier at a time.

This chapter isn't about dodging difficulty. You can't do that anyway. It's about learning to deal with problems without losing steam or ditching your dreams.

Dealing with Fear and Doubt

Fear and doubt are like those relatives who show up without calling first. You're about to make a big move, start something new, chase a dream with no guarantees; boom, there they are.

Here's the thing: you're never getting rid of them completely. The trick is keeping them from running your life.

Fear loves darkness. When you won't look at it directly, it seems huge and terrifying. But shine a light on what actually scares you, name it specifically instead of just feeling that general dread, and it usually shrinks down to something you can handle.

Imagine you are walking down a dark street and seeing a scary shadow. Your heart races until you get closer and realize it's just a trash can. Fear works the same way.

Doubt's trickier. It dresses up like wisdom. Sounds reasonable. Makes you question every move, plants confusion everywhere, and has you second-guessing decisions you already made.

Sure, thinking things through matters. But when you're stuck in analysis paralysis? That causes more trouble than just making a choice and tweaking it later if needed.

So what do you do when these feelings won't leave you alone?

First, call them out. What exactly are you afraid of? Break it down. Looking stupid? Getting rejected? Not knowing what comes next? Once you name it specifically, it stops being this huge, vague monster.

Do the same with doubt. Where's it coming from? Bad experiences from before? People giving you grief? Worrying about stuff that probably won't even happen? Figure out the source, and you can deal with it better.

Want to take fear's power away? Get prepared. Really prepared. When you know your stuff inside and out, fear loosens its grip big time. Knowledge and practice become your secret weapons.

Picture getting ready for a major presentation. You research everything, practice until you're sick of hearing yourself, and think through every possible question someone might throw at you. Suddenly, you're not dreading the unknown anymore; you're ready for whatever comes.

This works anywhere fear pops up: prepare like crazy, practice until it's automatic, then go do the thing.

Mental rehearsal is another game-changer. Not daydreaming, actual practice in your head.

Watch any pro athlete. They run through plays in their mind, see themselves making the moves, and imagine handling different scenarios. Their brain gets trained to recognize what's happening and respond under pressure. Confidence goes up, anxiety goes down.

Try it yourself. Got a tough conversation coming up? See it going smoothly in your mind. Big presentation? Walk through every slide mentally. Starting a new project? Picture yourself solving the problems you know will come up.

Your brain can't totally tell the difference between really vivid imagination and stuff that actually happened. Use that to your advantage.

Who and what you hang around with matters more than you think. Spend time with people and in places that push you forward, not drag you back.

Expose yourself less to toxic things and people, such as people who trash your dreams, places that kill your creativity, and habits that leave you exhausted. Instead, find mentors and friends who've got your back, groups where people actually want to see you win, and read stuff that fires you up instead of feeding your doubts.

Positive self-talk might feel weird at first, but it works. Telling yourself "I can handle whatever comes up" or "I trust my gut" sounds cheesy, I know. Keep at it though. Your thought patterns actually change over time.

Remember other times you were scared or unsure but did the thing anyway? Those are gold. Next time fear shows up, pull out those memories. You've beaten this before. You'll beat it again.

Breaking big goals into bite-sized pieces helps when everything feels overwhelming. Fear gets worse when your goal looks impossibly huge. When you break them down... each piece becomes less scary.

Ever put together a massive jigsaw puzzle? You don't dump all the thousand pieces out and try to do it all at once. You find the corners first. Then the edges. Fill in bit by bit. Same deal with scary goals, one manageable chunk at a time. Every little win makes you braver for the next one.

Tell someone you trust about your goals and worries. Saying fears out loud often makes them less powerful. Plus, having someone checking in on you keeps you from backing out. Pick someone who believes in you but will also call you on your BS when needed.

Here's what you need to accept: fear and doubt are permanent residents. They're human. The goal isn't making them disappear, it's moving forward anyway.

Real courage? That's being scared and doing it anyway. Treat fear and doubt like annoying travel companions. You can acknowledge they're there, feel them, and still keep walking.

Celebrate every win, even tiny ones. This builds a positive cycle that strengthens your belief in yourself. Made a hard call? Did something uncomfortable? Pushed through when you wanted to quit? That's worth recognizing.

These celebrations create a bank of good experiences you can withdraw from when fear and doubt come knocking again.

Fear and doubt aren't the bad guys in your story. They're the resistance that makes you stronger. Handle them right: through preparation, mental practice, good people around you, breaking things down, and patting yourself on the back, and they transform from brick walls into speed bumps.

Building Resilience

Life never gives you a straight shot from where you are to where you want to be. It throws curves, roadblocks, and detours that test how badly you want what you're after.

If you're going after anything that matters, problems aren't just possible, they're guaranteed. And honestly? They're usually what makes you grow. That's why resilience matters so much. It's what keeps you in the game when things get rough.

Resilience isn't about dodging punches. It's about taking the hit and getting back up stronger.

Picture learning to box. That first punch to the face? Shocking. But each one after that, you adjust your stance, tighten your defense, build your endurance. The hits still come, but they don't knock you down as easily. That's resilience, building your ability to take the punch and keep swinging.

Building this toughness isn't simple. You need grit, determination, and sometimes just plain stubbornness. But if you want to reignite that lost spark and chase what matters, you absolutely need it.

A huge part of resilience is keeping your head up when everything's going wrong. Not fake positivity where you pretend problems don't exist, but finding the opportunity hiding in the mess.

Got knocked back? What can you learn from it? Someone said no? How can you improve for next time? Missed your shot? What other doors might open instead?

Resilience means you never stop learning and adjusting. Problems rarely come alone; they bring lessons that help you level up.

Make it a habit to reflect. After something goes wrong, ask yourself what you gained from it. Did you find a new approach? Discover you're tougher than you thought? Come up with a better solution? These insights become tools for whatever comes next.

How you handle stress makes or breaks your resilience. Stress can either crush you or forge you—it depends on your approach.

Find what works for you. Maybe it's meditation, hitting the gym, keeping things in perspective, or finding the humor in ridiculous situations. Sometimes laughing at the absurdity of it all is the best medicine. Remember, resilience is both mental and physical; you need to take care of both.

Your surroundings affect how resilient you can be. Build spaces that help you grow. Get rid of what's poisoning your progress: negative people, bad habits, destructive thoughts.

Find people who both support and challenge you. Pick your fights carefully. Not every battle needs your energy.

Figure out what's worth the fight and what you should just walk away from.

Having a solid crew makes all the difference in building resilience. Being part of a supportive network gives you backup, encouragement, and fresh perspectives.

Look for groups that share your goals and values. When you're surrounded by people heading in the same direction, their strength adds to yours.

Sometimes the biggest resilience challenge is internal, the baseless stories you tell yourself about what you can and can't do.

Every time you think "I can't," stop and change it to "I'll try" or even better, "I will." The narrative in your head becomes your reality. Building resilience means rewriting those stories as much as facing external challenges.

Persistence is resilience's best friend. Starting is the easy part. Finishing when it gets hard? That takes something else entirely.

Think about running a marathon. Everyone takes off strong at the start. But the ones who cross the finish line? They pace themselves, ride out the ups and downs, and stay mentally tough. They just keep putting one foot in front of the other, even when the road seems endless.

Recognize small victories along the way. Every milestone counts.

Faced down a small fear today? Took one step toward that big goal? Those are wins. Noticing and celebrating these moments trains your brain to see progress instead of just focusing on what's still left to do.

Building resilience happens on multiple fronts. You need the right mindset, you need to keep learning, manage your stress, build the right environment, fix your internal dialogue, stick with it when it sucks, and celebrate the small stuff.

It's about gathering the tools and mindset to turn roadblocks into stepping stones. Every challenge you face, every win you earn, adds another layer of toughness, preparing you not just to survive future obstacles but to crush them.

That unbreakable spirit fueled by passion? It keeps your fire burning even when life tries to blow it out. That's the gift of resilience, the ability to keep chasing what matters to you, no matter what gets thrown in your path.

Chapter 6: The Role of Mindset

*"Whether you think you can, or you think you can't—
you're right."*

—Henry Ford

Your mindset isn't just how you think about things. It's like the operating system that runs everything else in your life.

Here's what's wild: two people can face the exact same situation: same setback, same opportunity, same challenge, and end up in completely different places. Not because one's smarter or more talented. They're just running different mental software.

One person hits a wall and thinks it's proof they should quit. The other sees it as a puzzle to solve. Same wall, different interpretation, totally different outcome.

That's the power of mindset.

When I decided to claw my way back from rock bottom, nothing had actually changed. Still had the same diagnosis, same empty bank account, same responsibilities weighing on me. What shifted wasn't my circumstances; it was how I looked at them.

Instead of thinking "I can't build anything because I'm sick," I started thinking "I'll figure out how to build something even though I'm sick." Tiny change in words, massive change in what became possible.

Let's dig into how mindset shapes everything else, and how you can adjust yours to support your goals rather than sabotage them.

Developing a Growth Mindset

Carol Dweck, who boiled mindset down to two basic types, fixed and growth, found something intriguing.

A fixed mindset believes your abilities are set in stone. You're either good at something, or you're not. Talent's something you're born with, intelligence is predetermined, and effort only gets you so far before you hit your natural ceiling.

A growth mindset believes that abilities can be developed. Sure, talent matters, but effort and learning matter way more. You're not stuck with what you've got right now; you can expand your capabilities through practice and persistence.[1]

Why should you care about this? Because it completely changes how you handle difficulty.

With a fixed mindset, challenges feel like threats to who you are. If you think you're either smart or you're not, then struggling with something feels like proof you're not. So you dodge challenges that might expose your limits. You stick to your comfort zone, where you already know you're good.

---

[1] Dweck, C. (2025, September 16). Carol Dweck revisits the "Growth Mindset" (Opinion). *Education Week.* https://www.edweek.org/leadership/opinion-carol-dweck-revisits-the-growth-mindset/2015/09

When you have a growth mindset, challenges are just information. Struggling means you're learning something new. Difficulty shows you're pushing past what you currently know, which is exactly how you get better. You actually seek out challenges because that's where the growth happens.

Think about picking up any new skill. At first, you're terrible. Everyone is. But people with fixed mindsets often quit right there. "Guess I'm just not good at this." People with growth mindsets push through that awkward beginner phase because they expect to suck at first. They know getting good comes later, after putting in the work.

The words you use, both out loud and in your head, show what kind of mindset you're working with, and they reinforce it too.

"I can't do this" is fixed mindset talk. It's declaring game over before you've really tried.

"I can't do this yet" is growth mindset talk. You're acknowledging where you are now while leaving the door open for where you could be.

You will see a notable difference when you say "I'm terrible at math" versus "I haven't figured out this math concept yet." "I failed" versus "I found out what doesn't work." "This is too hard" versus "This needs more effort than I've given it so far."

Remember that small word changes lead to big mindset shifts over time. Here's something to try: watch how you react when other people succeed.

A fixed mindset often feels threatened when others do well, especially in areas where you want to succeed. Their win somehow feels like your loss. Like, there's only so much success to go around.

A growth mindset sees other people's success as proof of what's possible. If they figured it out, maybe you can too. Their achievement actually expands what you think you're capable of instead of making you feel smaller.

This shows up big time in how you handle feedback.

Fixed mindset treats feedback like a verdict. Criticism feels like a personal attack. Even helpful suggestions trigger defensiveness because they suggest you're not already good enough.

A growth mindset treats feedback like data. Criticism just shows you the gap between where you are and where you want to be. Constructive input tells you exactly where to focus your effort.

When someone points out a mistake or suggests how to do better, that's gold if you're trying to improve. It only stings if you think your current ability defines your worth as a person.

Curiosity is huge for a growth mindset. When you're curious, you ask questions without worrying about looking stupid. You explore. You experiment. You try things you might bomb at because understanding how they work matters more than protecting your ego.

A fixed mindset avoids questions because asking reveals what you don't know. A growth mindset loves questions because they're the fastest route to filling in the gaps.

Picture starting a new project or challenge. Fixed mindset asks: Can I do this with what I've got right now? If the answer looks like no, you probably bail.

Growth mindset asks: Can I learn what I need to pull this off? If the answer seems like yes, you go for it.

Different questions lead to different actions, which lead to different lives.

Mistakes and failures really show which mindset you're operating from. A fixed mindset takes failure personally. "I failed, so I'm a failure." It feels permanent and all-encompassing.

A growth mindset sees failure as feedback about your approach. "That way didn't work, so let me try something else." It's specific to the situation and temporary.

This isn't just playing with words. It's the difference between giving up and trying again with a better strategy.

Here's the thing, though: you probably have a growth mindset in some areas and a fixed mindset in others. Most of us do.

Maybe you believe you can learn business skills through hard work, but think athletic ability is all genetics. Maybe you think artistic talent is something you're born with, but leadership skills can be developed.

Notice where you catch yourself thinking "I'm just not that kind of person" versus where you think "I haven't learned that yet." Those beliefs control what you're willing to try and how you react when it gets tough.

The good news is, the mindset isn't permanent. You can shift from fixed to growth in specific areas by deliberately changing how you think about ability in those areas.

Start catching your language and self-talk. When you hear yourself making fixed mindset statements, flip them to growth mindset alternatives.

Pick something you've always thought you "couldn't do" and deliberately practice it. Not to become world-class, just to prove to yourself that effort leads to improvement.

Watch your reaction to other people's wins. If you feel threatened or diminished, that's fixed mindset talking. Consciously reframe it. What does their success teach you about what you could achieve?

Celebrate effort and progress, not just results. A fixed mindset only cares about the final score. A growth mindset celebrates getting better, regardless of where you end up.

These small adjustments add up over time. You start defaulting to a growth mindset more automatically.

Challenges feel less scary. Feedback becomes more useful. Progress feels more possible.

And that changes everything about what you're willing to try and how you handle it when things get hard.

The Power of Positive Thinking

Positive thinking gets a bad rap sometimes. People think it means sticking your head in the sand or believing you can wish your way to success.

That's not what real positive thinking is about.

Real positive thinking means interpreting situations in ways that open doors rather than slam them shut. It's choosing explanations that keep you moving forward instead of being stuck in place.

Two people get the same bad news. One sees it as proof they should give up. The other sees it as information about what to try next. Same news, different interpretation, different next move.

That's not ignoring reality. It's choosing which part of reality to focus on and what story to tell yourself about it.

Think about waking up tomorrow morning. You can focus on everything that's going to suck, all the problems waiting for you, all the work ahead, all the ways things might go wrong. Or you can focus on the opportunities, problems you get to solve, skills you'll build, progress you might make.

Same day ahead. Different focus. Completely different energy going into it.

This matters more than you'd think. Your brain responds to how you frame things. Frame them as threats, and your body goes into stress mode. Frame them as challenges you can handle, and your problem-solving mode kicks in instead.

Positive thinking doesn't mean forcing yourself to be happy about crappy situations. It means looking for the angle you can work with, what can you actually do here?

Lost a big client? Negative thinking fixates on the loss, the money gone, the rejection. Positive thinking asks what you can learn from why they left and how to use that to keep your other clients happier.

Screwed something up? Negative thinking spirals into beating yourself up about being an idiot. Positive thinking pulls out the lesson and uses it to avoid the same screw-up next time.

You're not pretending the problem doesn't exist. You're choosing to focus on the part you can actually do something about.

Research keeps showing that positive thinking leads to better outcomes, but here's why: it's not magic. It's practical.

When you think positively, you're more likely to take action. More likely to spot opportunities. More likely to keep going when things suck. Those behaviors create better results.

When you think negatively, you're more likely to give up, miss opportunities, and stop trying. Those behaviors create worse results.

The thinking shapes what you do, and what you do shapes what you get.

Gratitude practices work this way. When you regularly notice what's working instead of only what's broken, you train your brain to see the good stuff too. Problems don't disappear, but your view becomes more balanced, so you're not only seeing what's wrong.

That balanced view leads to better decisions because you're working with the full picture.

Visualization works the same way. When you mentally rehearse success, you're not magically making it happen. You're preparing your brain to recognize opportunities and execute the moves that lead there.

Athletes do this all the time: imagining perfect plays, smooth movements, nailing their performance. This mental practice translates to better actual performance because your brain processes vivid imagination almost like real experience.

You can use this for anything. Before a tough conversation, visualize it going well. Before starting a challenging project, see yourself handling it like a pro. This mental prep actually improves how you perform.

However, positive thinking requires staying honest about reality. Toxic positivity, pretending everything's rainbows when it's actually a dumpster fire, creates problems because you're not dealing with what's actually happening.

Real positive thinking admits problems exist while believing solutions are possible. That's totally different from denying problems exist.

The difference matters. One keeps you stuck in fantasy land. The other gets you moving to fix what's actually broken.

Pay attention to your explanatory style: how you explain why things happen.

When something goes wrong, do you blame permanent, personal, all-encompassing causes? "I'm not good enough, never will be, everything's going to fail." That creates learned helplessness and keeps you passive.

Or do you see temporary, specific, fixable causes? "That particular approach didn't work, so I'll try something different for this specific situation." That creates realistic optimism and gets you problem-solving.

Same event, different explanation, different response.

You can train yourself toward better explanatory styles by examining how you interpret setbacks. When something doesn't work, ask yourself: Is this really forever or just right now? Is this about me as a person or about this specific attempt? Is everything ruined or just this one thing?

Usually, setbacks are temporary, specific, and fixable. But negative thinking automatically jumps to permanent, personal, and pervasive. Catching that pattern and correcting it changes how you respond.

Who you hang around with matters here, too. Not people who deny reality, but people who approach challenges constructively.

If everyone around you focuses on why things can't work, that becomes your default setting. If people around you focus on how things might work despite the obstacles, that becomes your default instead.

This isn't about avoiding anyone who ever vents or has a bad day. It's about the overall balance of influences shaping how you think.

Positive thinking also makes relationships better. When you assume people mean well instead of jumping to the worst conclusion, you create space for real connection. When problems come up, seeing them as puzzles to solve together instead of proving the relationship is doomed leads to actually fixing things.

Here's the practical truth: positive thinking isn't about denying reality or faking happiness. It's about focusing on what you can do something about, interpreting setbacks in ways that keep you going, and believing solutions exist even when you can't see them yet.

That mindset, combined with actual work and smart strategy, creates way better outcomes than negative thinking with the same work and strategy.

Your thoughts don't magically create your reality. But they heavily influence your actions, and your actions absolutely create your reality.

Choose thoughts that support the actions you need to take and the outcomes you want to create. It's that straightforward.

Chapter 7: The Balance Between Work and Passion

"You can't pour from an empty cup."

—Unknown

The thing nobody is going to tell you is about chasing your goals. You must know when you're chasing goals. The thing that drives you can also destroy you if you're not careful.

Passion has the power to get you moving when logic says quit. It keeps you working when everyone else has gone home. It pushes you through obstacles that would stop someone who's just going through the motions.

But that same intensity can burn you out if you don't manage it properly.

After my diagnosis, after that ATM moment, I threw everything into building my business. Every waking hour. Every ounce of energy. Four kids to support, bills piling up, body not cooperating, I figured the answer was just work harder, push more, sleep less.

Know what happened? I hit a wall. Hard.

Not the kind where you're tired and need a weekend off, but where you just can't get out of bed. Where the thing you were passionate about suddenly feels like chains instead of wings.

That's burnout. And it's real.

Here I am going to talk about finding the right balance between pursuing what matters and maintaining the capacity to keep pursuing it. The first thing is to understand that working smart is important than working hard. Not dampening passion, but channeling it sustainably.

Because if you burn out chasing your goals, you don't get to enjoy achieving them.

Avoiding Burnout

Burnout surrounds you in a way that you are just done with everything, and that's what makes it dangerous. You're not fine one day and completely burned out the next. It's gradual. Small signs you ignore because you're too busy, too committed, too close to a breakthrough to slow down now.

First sign? Chronic exhaustion that can't be fixed by sleep. You wake up tired even after getting eight hours of sleep.

Second sign? Detachment. Things that used to excite you feel like obligations. Work you were passionate about becomes just work. People you care about start feeling like interruptions.

Third sign? Everything irritates you. Small problems feel massive. People asking reasonable questions feel like they're attacking you. Your patience disappears.

You're already exhausted or burning yourself out if you have any such experiences, and it is time to make changes before you crash completely.

One major cause? Lack of boundaries between work and everything else.

When you're passionate about something, the boundaries are not noticeable enough. It specifically applies to when you are building something for yourself. You work late because you want to. You work weekends because the project is interesting. You answer emails at midnight because you're thinking about the business anyway.

That works for short bursts. Sprints toward specific goals. But sustained over months or years? It destroys you.

I learned this the expensive way. Working eighty-hour weeks, convinced that if I just pushed harder, I'd break through. What actually happened was my body started failing more. I messed up my relationship with my kids because I wasn't mentally present with them. I was physically there, but in my mind, I was somewhere else. My work quality also decreased because I was too exhausted to think clearly.

The solution isn't necessarily working less. It's setting boundaries that protect your capacity to keep working.

For me, that meant no work after 7 p.m. unless it's a genuine emergency. Weekends are for family, not email. When I'm with my kids, my phone stays in my pocket.

Did this slow my business growth? Maybe slightly. Did it let me sustain the effort long-term without destroying myself? Absolutely.

You've got to decide what your boundaries are and then actually enforce them. Not just announce them and then ignore them when things get busy. Actually protect them like they matter.

Sleep isn't negotiable. I know you've heard this before. Everyone knows sleep matters. But there are many people who don't prioritize it. Sleep deprivation kills your cognitive function, your emotional regulation, your physical health, and your decision-making ability.

You're not being productive by sleeping less. You're being stupid.

I had to learn this too. I thought I could function on five hours. And it turned out I was just functioning poorly and never noticed it. My work quality and mood improved when I started working seven hours. And, I actually got more done in less time because my brain worked properly.

Physical health matters more than most people realize when sustaining passion. When your body feels terrible, maintaining enthusiasm for anything becomes difficult.

You don't need to become an athlete. But moving regularly, eating food that actually nourishes you instead of just filling you up, managing stress through exercise or whatever works for you, these aren't luxuries. They are requirements for sustained high performance.

I've MS, and my body doesn't cooperate even on good days. That left me with no choice, and I had to take care of my physical health.

You can also do that by finding what works for your situation and making it part of your routine.

Another critical piece: saying no.

When you're building something, opportunities appear. Projects, partnerships, speaking engagements, and new clients all sound good. All of it could be valuable. But you can't do everything, as it burns you out.

Learning to say no to good opportunities so you can say yes to great ones, that's a skill that takes practice. But it's essential.

I've turned down projects and rejected partnerships that looked attractive on paper but wouldn't spare me emotionally or mentally. Each time, it felt like walking away from money or opportunity.

But saying no to those things protected the capacity to say yes to better things. And it kept me from overloading to the point of collapse.

Your environment matters too. It is going to affect you if you're surrounded by people who drain your energy.

You might not be able to cut every toxic person out of your life, but you *can* create some distance. You can decide how much access they get to your time, your energy, and your peace of mind.

And while you're doing that, start spending more time with the people who lift you up, the ones who understand your goals, respect your focus, and actually add something positive to your life.

Good time management helps too because it helps you use the ones you already have in a way that actually serves you. Personally, I rely on time blocking and setting aside specific chunks of time for different kinds of work. It keeps me grounded and stops the chaos from taking over.

Deep work gets morning blocks when my brain functions best. Meetings and calls get afternoon blocks. Administrative stuff gets specific slots instead of randomly interrupting all day.

This isn't rigid scheduling where every minute is planned. It's creating a structure that protects focus and prevents the constant task-switching that exhausts your brain.

One more thing about burnout: celebrate small wins regularly.

Sometimes it feels like you aren't making any progress when you're just focusing on big goals. But that creates a psychological pattern where nothing feels good enough, nothing feels worth celebrating, and the whole journey becomes a grinding obligation.

Acknowledge progress. Completed a project phase? Recognize it. Had a good conversation with a potential client? Note it. Stuck to your boundaries for a week? That counts.

These small celebrations matter and make you believe that you're moving forward and progressing.

Burnout isn't inevitable. It's the result of unsustainable practices that have continued for too long. Change the practices, and you can maintain intensity without destroying yourself in the process.

Maintaining Passion in a Busy World

Life doesn't slow down to let you pursue passion. It keeps moving, demanding attention, creating obligations, filling every available minute with something that needs doing.

So how do you maintain passion when you're genuinely busy with legitimate responsibilities?

Not by finding more time, that's not happening. By making better use of the time you have.

Start with micro-moments. Small pockets of time throughout your day that currently go to nothing or to mindless scrolling.

Waiting for coffee? That's five minutes you could spend capturing ideas related to your passion project. Commuting? Time for a podcast or audiobook relevant to what you're building. Standing in line? Review your goals, plan your next steps, and do something that moves you forward even slightly.

These tiny increments add up significantly over weeks and months. You're not finding hours; you're reclaiming minutes that were wasted anyway.

But beyond micro-moments, you've got to actually schedule passion time like you schedule everything else that matters.

Here's what most people do: handle all their obligations first, then use whatever energy and time remains for passion projects. The problem is, there's rarely anything remaining. Obligations expand to fill available space.

Flip it. Schedule your passion work first, treat it as non-negotiable as any important meeting, and fit other things around it.

When I was building my business while managing MS and raising four kids, I didn't have extra time lying around. So I protected morning hours before the kids woke up. That time was mine. Not for email, not for putting out fires, not for anything except moving my business forward.

Was it convenient? No. Did I want to wake up at 5 a.m. every day? Definitely not. But that protected time made everything else possible.

You've got to find your equivalent and then actually defend it. Not just when it's easy, but especially when everything else is demanding attention.

Another approach is to find synergy between your work and your passion.

Passionate about writing but working in finance? Look for opportunities to write articles, contribute to company communications, and create content related to your industry.

Love creative problem-solving but stuck in routine work? Volunteer for projects that need innovative thinking.

You're not always going to find perfect overlap, but often there's more room for integration than people realize. Look for it actively instead of assuming work and passion must be completely separate.

Physical and mental health protect your ability to maintain passion. When you're exhausted, when your body hurts, when stress has fried your nervous system, maintaining enthusiasm for anything becomes nearly impossible.

So, exercise, sleep, nutrition, and stress management aren't separate from maintaining passion. They're foundational to it.

I've had days where my MS symptoms flare and everything physical becomes difficult. On those days, maintaining passion for my work is hard. I push through because I have to, but it costs more energy than when I'm managing my health well.

Taking care of yourself isn't selfish or indulgent. It's practical maintenance that protects your capacity to pursue what matters.

Technology can help or hurt in maintaining passion. Your phone provides tools that could help you stay organized, learn faster, and connect with the community. It also provides infinite distraction that fragments your attention and drains the time you could use productively.

Use technology deliberately. Apps that support your goals, yes. Mindless scrolling that eats hours, no. Set boundaries around digital consumption the same way you set boundaries around everything else.

Community and accountability matter enormously for maintaining passion when life is busy.

When you're part of a group pursuing similar goals, their energy reinforces yours. When you've committed publicly to specific actions, you're more likely to follow through even when motivation dips.

Find your people. Share your goals. Create structures where you're accountable to more than just yourself.

I meet monthly with other business owners. We review progress, share challenges, and push each other forward. That external accountability keeps me moving during periods when internal motivation alone wouldn't be enough.

Don't underestimate downtime either. Your brain needs space to process, to make connections, to recharge.

Constant activity, constant productivity, constant forward motion, that doesn't actually maximize output. It exhausts you and reduces quality.

Build in actual rest. Sometimes, you just need a walk without a podcast in your ears or sitting without checking your phone. Let your thoughts wander a bit.

You must know when and how to say no on purpose. Protect your time and energy; they're not unlimited. Most of the stuff that feels urgent isn't really that important anyway.

And don't expect to feel "on fire" all the time. Some days you'll be in the zone; other days you'll wonder why you're even doing this. Both are normal. Both pass. What matters is that you keep showing up.

I've had days when I questioned everything, whether the business was worth it, whether I was even making progress. But I kept going, even when I didn't feel like it. Looking back, that consistency made all the difference.

Staying passionate in a busy world isn't about always being motivated. It's about doing the work, even when you're not. You don't find perfect balance once, and you keep it forever; you keep adjusting as life shifts, but the basics never change. That's how you actually make it.

Chapter 8: Taking Action

"The secret of getting ahead is getting started."

—Mark Twain

Everything we have discussed up to this point, such as understanding passion, setting goals, building support, and managing balance… none of it matters if you don't do anything with it.

I know it may sound harsh. But it's true.

When you gain knowledge but don't take any action, it is just taking up space in your head. Similarly, plans without execution are just fantasies. Good intentions without follow-through don't change anything.

After my ATM moment, I had clarity about what I needed to do. Build a business. Support my family. Prove that my diagnosis wasn't the end of my story. Great. Very motivating.

But between that clarity and actual results? Thousands of hours of work. Small actions repeated consistently. Days when I didn't feel like showing up but did anyway.

People get stuck when they don't know the gap between Tha knowing what to do and actually doing it. It is not because they lack information or ability. It is because taking action is hard, and not taking action is even easier.

This chapter is about closing that gap. Building the daily practices that turn intentions into outcomes. Understanding why we avoid action and how to move forward anyway.

Because at some point, you've got to stop preparing and start executing.

The Importance of Daily Habits

Big achievements sound impressive when you describe them. Built a successful business. Wrote a book. Lost fifty pounds. Learned a new skill.

But here's what actually creates those achievements: small actions repeated so consistently they become automatic.

Not dramatic gestures. Not occasional bursts of intense effort. These are simple daily habits that provide bigger results over time.

Your brain forms habits in the basal ganglia. It is the same region that processes emotions and recognizes patterns. Your brain creates neural pathways that make that action easier and more automatic over time when we repeat an action.

This is why breaking bad habits feels difficult: you're fighting established neural patterns. And why good habits, once formed, eventually require less conscious effort. They've become encoded in your brain's operating system.

Most people who reach big goals don't just get there through talent or luck. They make routines that line up with what they want and stick with them.

Think about how small things add up over time. Reading for twenty minutes today won't turn you into an expert, but doing it every day will move you a lot closer than doing nothing at all.

One workout doesn't transform your health. Writing two hundred words doesn't complete a book.

But reading twenty minutes daily for a year? That's over a hundred hours of learning. Working out three times weekly for a year? That's a major physical transformation. Writing two hundred words daily? That's a seventy-thousand-word book in a year.

The actions themselves are manageable. Almost trivially small. Over time, doing the same small things again and again starts to add up in ways that don't seem possible.

When I decided to grow my business, I had to get clear on what actions would work. Not the "when I have time" kind of tasks, but the ones I could do right now, and keep doing every day.

For me, that meant spending the first two hours after waking up on business development, before anything else could get in the way.

Not checking email. Not putting out fires. Just focused work on building what I was trying to create.

Some days, those two hours felt incredibly productive. Other days, they felt like slogging through mud. But over months and years, those daily sessions built something substantial.

That's how habits work. Individual sessions don't feel transformative. The pattern of consistent sessions creates transformation.

Your habits also affect your mental state, and it goes beyond the tasks. Waking at the same time daily regulates your circadian rhythm. It influences energy levels, focus, and emotional stability. Regular exercise affects our brain in many ways, such as improving mood and cognitive function.

These aren't just productivity hacks. They're foundational practices that determine whether you can sustain effort over time or burn out trying.

Here's the practical challenge with habits: starting them requires conscious effort, and maintaining them requires consistency even when motivation is absent.

The two-minute rule helps with starting. If a habit can be done in two minutes, do it immediately. Want to start running? Put on running shoes. That's the two-minute version. Once shoes are on, starting the actual run becomes more likely.

Want to build a writing habit? Write one sentence. That's the two-minute version. Once you've written one sentence, continuing becomes easier.

The point isn't completing your entire goal in two minutes. It's lowering the activation energy required to start, which is usually the hardest part.

For maintaining habits when motivation fades, and it will fade, accountability helps enormously. Tell someone your commitment. Join a group pursuing similar goals. Create external structures that make skipping harder than following through.

I meet with other business owners a lot. We share our plans and progress. That external accountability keeps me moving during periods when internal motivation alone wouldn't be enough.

Also recognize that perfection isn't the goal. Consistency is. Miss a day? Get back to it the next day. Breaking your streak doesn't erase the habit; only an extended absence does.

Some days, I couldn't do my full two-hour morning session because my MS symptoms flared or something with the kids required immediate attention. Those breaks didn't destroy the habit because I returned to it consistently.

The habit isn't about perfect execution. It's about the overall pattern of showing up repeatedly.

The not-so-great habits deserve attention, too. If you're always reaching for your phone, that's a pattern getting in the way of your focus. If you keep putting things off, that's a habit fighting against the progress you're trying to make.

You can't just stack good habits on top of bad ones and hope for the best. The unhelpful ones need to be replaced or made harder to repeat. For me, that meant literally moving my phone out of sight during work hours. If it were nearby, I'd end up checking it without even thinking. Once it was out of reach, staying focused got a lot easier.

Your daily habits are what connect where you are to where you want to be. They're not flashy or exciting, but they're what actually move the needle. So pick the ones that match your goals and build from there.

Start them using two-minute versions. Build accountability structures. Return to them consistently even after breaks. Address competing bad habits that undermine progress.

Do that, and over time, you'll look back and realize that those small daily actions have built something substantial.

Procrastination and How to Beat It

Procrastination kills more dreams than failure ever will.

Failure at least means you tried. Procrastination means you never got started, or you started but kept delaying the hard parts until momentum died completely.

Everyone procrastinates sometimes. The question is whether you let it control your actions or whether you develop strategies to move forward despite it.

The first step is understanding why you're procrastinating. It's rarely about being lazy. Usually, it's about fear, being overwhelmed, or being unclear about the next steps.

Fear of failure makes starting feel dangerous. If you don't try, you can't fail. If you do try and fail, that confirms your worst thoughts about yourself. So procrastination becomes protection against potential failure.

Feeling overwhelmed usually hits when a goal looks too big to handle. You don't know where to start, everything feels urgent, and before you know it. You're frozen.

A lot of procrastination comes from that same place. You know what you want, but not what to do next. The big picture is clear, the next step isn't, and that uncertainty makes it easy to stall.

Different kinds of procrastination need different fixes.

If fear is the thing holding you back, start by changing how you think about failure. Every successful person has a trail of failures behind them. Failing doesn't mean you're not capable, it just means you're testing ideas, learning what doesn't work so you can find what does.

I've had plenty of flops myself. Business strategies that went nowhere. Client projects that fell apart. Ideas that sounded brilliant one day and completely foolish the next. None of that meant I was a failure. It only meant I'd crossed a few wrong turns off the map.

That mindset doesn't make fear disappear, but it makes it manageable. When you see failure as information instead of judgment, you stop freezing up every time something doesn't go perfectly.

If the problem is overwhelming, the answer is to shrink the goal down until it feels doable. Don't try to take on the whole project at once. Just pick one small, specific action you can handle today.

When I first started my business, the entire thing felt impossible. But I could make one phone call to one potential client. That single step felt achievable. Do that enough times, and you end up building something big without ever having to carry the whole weight of it at once.

And if you're stuck because you simply don't know what to do next, pause and get clear before you try to act. Ask yourself, *What exactly needs to happen right now?* Not later—right now. If you can't answer that, you'll just keep spinning and feeling guilty for not moving forward.

Sometimes the next step is doing a bit of research. Sometimes it's asking for help. Sometimes it's finally making a decision you've been avoiding. Whatever it is, name it clearly so you can take real action instead of staying stuck in your head.

The "perfect time" trap causes enormous procrastination. You're waiting for conditions to be ideal before starting. More time available, more knowledge acquired, more resources accumulated, more certainty about the right approach.

Perfect conditions never arrive. There's always something imperfect about the current moment. If you wait for perfection, you wait forever.

The best time to start is now, with whatever you currently have available. Not because now is perfect, but because now is what you've got, and waiting doesn't improve it.

I didn't start my business under ideal conditions. I was dealing with a chronic illness, raising four kids, had limited capital, and didn't know everything I needed to know. Starting anyway with those limitations was the only way forward.

Waiting for better conditions would have meant never starting at all.

Accountability structures help overcome procrastination significantly. When you've committed to someone else that you'll complete something by a certain time, you're more likely to follow through.

Not because you're afraid of judgment necessarily. Because external commitment adds structure that internal commitment alone often lacks.

I told my accountability group I'd reach out to ten potential clients that month. Did I want to make those calls? Not particularly. But I'd committed publicly, so I did it anyway.

The environment affects procrastination, too. If your workspace is full of distractions, if your phone constantly interrupts you, if noise and chaos surround you, then focusing on difficult tasks becomes impossible.

To overcome this, remove distractions and set boundaries around interruptions. Make the hard thing easier to do.

I can't work productively with notifications popping up on my phone screen constantly. So during focused work time, the phone goes in another room. No interruptions are allowed except for genuine emergencies.

That environmental structure makes procrastination harder and productivity easier.

Also recognize that motivation follows action more often than it precedes it. You don't wait until you feel motivated to start. You start, and motivation often appears after you're already moving.

I don't always feel motivated to work when my alarm goes off at 5 AM. But I start anyway, and usually within twenty minutes, I'm engaged and productive. If I waited to feel motivated first, I'd skip most mornings.

Reward systems help too. When you complete difficult tasks, give yourself something you enjoy. Not as bribery exactly, but as positive reinforcement that trains your brain to associate productivity with pleasure.

My reward system is simple: after completing my morning work session, I get coffee and time to read something unrelated to work. That reward makes the difficult morning work feel worth doing.

Finally, embrace imperfection. Procrastination often stems from perfectionism; if you can't do something perfectly, you'd rather not do it at all.

But perfect is the enemy of done. Progress matters more than perfection. Starting imperfectly beats not starting at all.

My first attempts at business development were clumsy. My early client presentations weren't polished. My initial service offerings needed refinement.

All of that was fine. Imperfect action beats perfect inaction every time.

Procrastination will always be there, offering reasons to delay. Your job isn't eliminating it completely. Your job is recognizing when it's operating and choosing to act anyway.

Understand why you're procrastinating. Break large tasks into manageable pieces. Start now instead of waiting for perfect conditions. Build accountability. Control your environment. Focus on completion over perfection.

Do that consistently, and you'll move forward despite procrastination instead of waiting for it to magically disappear.

Because it won't disappear. You just stop letting it control whether you act.

Chapter 9: Reclaiming Lost Passion

"It is never too late to be what you might have been."

—George Eliot

Most people lose touch with what they once cared about deeply.

Not dramatically. Just gradually, as life accumulates responsibilities, obligations, and practical necessities that crowd out activities done purely because they mattered.

You had interests once. Things you did because you wanted to, not because you had to. Things that engaged you fully, where time disappeared because you were absorbed in the activity itself.

Then life happened. Career demands. Family responsibilities. Financial pressures. Health challenges. The slow accumulation of must-dos leaves little space for want-to-dos.

Eventually, you look up and realize years have passed since you engaged with anything purely because it interested you. Everything's become an obligation or a necessity. Nothing's just because you care about it.

That loss matters more than people often recognize. Not because hobbies are sacred, but because losing connection with what genuinely interests you creates a life that's all responsibility and no satisfaction.

You can function that way. Many people do. But functioning isn't the same as living fully.

This chapter is about recognizing when you've lost connection with what matters to you personally and figuring out how to reclaim it. Not through dramatic life overhauls necessarily, but through deliberate small actions that reconnect you with interests and activities that got buried under life's demands.

Sustainable success requires more than just achieving professional goals. It requires maintaining a connection with what makes you feel alive beyond accomplishments and obligations.

Rediscovering What You Love

Figuring out what you've lost connection with requires an honest assessment of what you once cared about and why you stopped.

For me, after my MS diagnosis and during early business-building years, almost everything became survival-focused. Work consumed available energy. Managing illness took the rest. Everything else fell away.

That was necessary temporarily. Crisis periods require triage—focusing on essentials, letting non-essentials go.

But "temporarily" stretched into years. I wasn't just managing a crisis anymore, but I'd completely lost connection with activities I'd once enjoyed. Reading for pleasure, not just business learning. Physical activity beyond the minimum needed for health. Time with friends not connected to work.

Recognizing that loss required stepping back and honestly assessing what my life had become. All work, all management, no activities done purely because they interested me.

Start your assessment by thinking about what you used to do before current responsibilities dominated everything. Not necessarily childhood interests, though those count, but any period when you had activities you pursued because you wanted to, not because you had to.

What were those activities? Why did they matter to you? What about them engaged you?

Sometimes the specific activity isn't what matters. It's the underlying need that the activity fulfilled. Maybe you loved playing music. The specific need might have been creative expression, or social connection through playing with others, or satisfaction from developing a skill.

Understanding the underlying need helps because you might not be able to resume the exact same activity. But you can find different activities fulfilling the same need.

I can't do many physical activities I once enjoyed because MS affects coordination and stamina. But understanding that I needed physical activity for mental clarity and stress management helped me find adapted activities that serve the same function.

Give yourself permission to explore without immediate pressure to become good at anything or achieve results. The exploration phase is about discovering what still interests you, not about performing.

This feels awkward often. Revisiting old interests after years away means starting over to some degree. You won't be as capable as you once were. That's fine. The point isn't recapturing past performance. It's reconnecting with what the activity offers now.

I started reading fiction again after years of only reading business books. Felt indulgent at first, like I should be doing something more productive. But that reading provided a mental reset that improved everything else. Sometimes "unproductive" activities are actually essential maintenance.

Your environment affects reconnection significantly. If you're surrounded only by work-related materials and reminders of obligations, passionate activities feel out of place.

Create physical space for activities you're trying to reconnect with. A visible musical instrument is more likely to get played than one buried in a closet. Art supplies left out get used more than supplies stored away.

This doesn't necessarily require a dedicated room. Just a visible presence that reminds you these activities exist and are available.

Talk to people who knew you before everything became obligation-focused. They might remember interests and enthusiasms you've forgotten. Those conversations can surface possibilities you're no longer aware of.

Your passions may have evolved. You're not the person you were years ago. What interested you then might not interest you now. That's normal.

Look for evolved versions of old interests. Maybe you once loved working with your hands, building things. Now that might manifest as a different type of making: cooking, gardening, programming, whatever. Core interest in creating tangible results remains, but specific expression changes.

Timing matters. You probably can't suddenly devote hours daily to rediscovered interests. Life still has demands. Start small. Even fifteen minutes daily reconnects you with activity in ways that finding "someday when I have time" never does.

I started with morning reading, just twenty minutes before the day began. That small, consistent practice reconnected me with reading for pleasure after years of treating it as purely utilitarian.

Consider combining old interests with new approaches or technologies. Maybe you loved photography, but film processing seems antiquated. Digital photography offers different possibilities while maintaining a core interest in capturing images.

That modernization can make old interests feel fresh instead of nostalgic.

Use accumulated experience and wisdom to deepen engagement. You understand things now that you didn't earlier. That understanding can create a richer appreciation for activities you're revisiting.

When I returned to physical activity after being forced away by illness, I approached it differently than in my younger years. Less about performance, more about maintaining capability and mental health. That shift made it sustainable in ways an earlier approach wouldn't have been.

Sometimes old activities don't resonate anymore. That's information, not failure. Maybe your interests genuinely changed. Explore different directions instead of forcing dead activity.

Connect with others who share the interests you're exploring. Online communities, local groups, and classes provide both knowledge and motivation. Seeing other people engaged with what interests you reinforces that it's a worthwhile pursuit.

After starting to write more, I connected with other writers. That community provided both practical help and encouragement during periods when writing felt like a questionable use of time.

Revisit past achievements related to interests you're reconnecting with. Not to live in the past, but to remember you once cared enough about this to develop the capability. That reminder can overcome the initial awkwardness of starting again.

Small investments can catalyze reconnection. New equipment, updated tools, taking class, these signal to yourself that this interest matters, not just leftover from the past.

But don't let equipment become an excuse. "I'll start when I have the right setup" often means never starting. Begin with what's available. Upgrade as engagement justifies investment.

Understand that rediscovering what you love isn't a linear process with a clear endpoint. It's an ongoing exploration that meanders. Some interests will stick. Others won't. That's the point of exploring, discovering what actually matters now versus what you think should matter.

Give yourself permission for this exploration to take time. You're rebuilding connection severed by years of necessary focus on survival and obligation. That reconnection happens gradually through consistent small actions, not sudden breakthroughs.

The goal isn't adding more obligations to an already-full life. It's reclaiming space for activities that restore you rather than deplete you. Activities done because you want to, not because you should.

That reclamation is essential maintenance, not luxury. Without connection to what interests you beyond obligations and achievements, sustained high performance becomes impossible. You need activities that restore energy, not just consume it.

Start exploring. Notice what creates genuine interest versus what you think should interest you. Follow actual interest, even if it seems impractical or unimpressive. Small, consistent engagement compounds over time into a reconnection that enriches everything else.

Strategies for Rekindling Passion

Once you've identified what you've lost connection with, rekindling it requires deliberate strategy.

Passive wishfulness doesn't reconnect you with lost interests. You need active approaches that create space and momentum for activities you're trying to reclaim.

Start by examining what got you interested originally. What about this activity engaged you? Understanding original appeal helps recreate conditions that support engagement now.

I loved reading as a kid because it provided an escape and access to ideas beyond my immediate environment. As an adult, reading still serves those functions but also provides perspective and a mental reset from daily demands. Understanding both the original and current appeal helps protect time for it.

The environment shapes behavior powerfully. If your environment only supports work and obligations, passionate activities won't happen regardless of intentions.

Deliberately create environmental support for activities you're rekindling. This might mean dedicated space, visible materials, scheduled time, whatever removes friction between intention and action.

I keep books visible and accessible. When I have fifteen minutes between tasks, I can pick one up immediately instead of needing to retrieve it from somewhere. That ease matters enormously for actual engagement versus theoretical interest.

Sometimes, pursuing a completely new interest catalyzes passion in other areas. New activity provides fresh energy and perspective that transfers to existing interests.

After my diagnosis, I started learning about topics completely unrelated to work or health management. That learning for its own sake rekindled intellectual curiosity that had become purely utilitarian. That broader curiosity then enhanced work thinking too.

Community amplifies individual effort. Connecting with others engaged in activities you're rekindling provides both practical help and motivation.

Online forums, local groups, classes—these create accountability and shared enthusiasm that sustains effort when individual motivation flags.

I joined a running group after years of solo exercise. The social component transformed the activity from an obligation into something I looked forward to. That shift from "should do" to "want to do" mattered enormously for sustainability.

Set small achievable goals related to your passion activities. Not performance goals necessarily, but engagement goals. "Practice guitar three times this week" rather than "master this piece."

Those small goals create a sense of progress that builds momentum. Achieving them reinforces that this activity is happening, not just something you intend to do someday.

Celebrate small wins. Completed a fifteen-minute practice session. Read a chapter of a book. Spent the afternoon on a hobby project. These small engagements matter. Acknowledging them reinforces behavior.

Reflect regularly on progress and growth. Not just in passion activities themselves, but in how engaging with them affects everything else. A better mood, clearer thinking, and increased energy; these effects justify the time investment.

I track how consistent physical activity affects both MS symptoms and work productivity. Seeing that connection helps prioritize exercise when competing demands make it feel expendable.

Consider finding a mentor who is already engaged in the activity you're rekindling. Their experience offers both practical guidance and evidence that sustained engagement is achievable.

Mentors don't need to be in formal relationships. Following people online, reading about their practices, and learning from their approaches provides guidance and motivation.

Physical health affects energy available for everything, including passion pursuits. Poor sleep, inadequate nutrition, and insufficient movement drain the capacity for engaging with anything beyond the bare necessities.

Protecting basic health maintenance creates a foundation for rekindling passion. Hard to reconnect with interests when you're constantly exhausted or physically compromised.

Be honest about what's preventing engagement. Sometimes it's not a lack of time or energy. It's other factors: toxic relationships, unsatisfying work, and unaddressed problems, that drain enthusiasm for everything.

Addressing those underlying issues might be necessary before passion activities can take root. If daily life is actively draining, adding positive activities won't solve fundamental problems.

This doesn't mean wait for perfect conditions. But recognize when obstacles are environmental versus motivational. Environmental obstacles need to be addressed directly rather than just trying harder.

Small acts of self-kindness support passion rekindling. Taking breaks. Saying no to demands that aren't actually necessary. Allowing unstructured time. Treating yourself like someone whose well-being matters.

Passion withers when life is constant grinding. Creating space for rest and recovery isn't indulgence; it's maintenance that enables sustained engagement with what matters.

Mindfulness helps maintain a connection with activities while doing them. Actually being present during a passionate activity, rather than mentally somewhere else, makes fifteen minutes feel substantial instead of rushed.

I practice this with reading. When I'm reading, I'm reading, not also checking messages or thinking about work problems. That full presence makes short reading periods satisfying in ways that longer, but distracted, periods never were.

Practice curiosity about what you're discovering. Approach rekindling passion as exploration rather than a return to known territory. You've changed. The activity might reveal different dimensions than you remember.

That curiosity prevents disappointment when things don't feel exactly like they did years ago. Of course they don't. You're different now. The question isn't whether it matches memory, but whether it offers something valuable now.

Protect time for passion activities like you protect important work commitments. If it's not scheduled, other demands will consume available time. Schedule it. Honor that commitment like you would honor meeting with an important person.

Because it is meeting with an important person, yourself, engaging with what matters to you beyond obligations.

Rekindling passion requires patience. A connection severed by years of neglect doesn't restore instantly. But consistent small engagement rebuilds that connection steadily.

Some weeks, you'll feel progress. Other weeks, you'll wonder why you're bothering. Long-term trend matters more than any individual session. Keep showing up. The reconnection happens through accumulated engagement, not a single breakthrough moment.

Understand that this isn't adding to an already full life. It's reclaiming what makes a full life feel worthwhile, rather than just exhausting. Activities that restore energy rather than deplete it. Engagement that reminds you there's more to existence than meeting obligations.

That reclamation is essential, not optional. Without connection to what interests you beyond accomplishments and duties, everything becomes grinding. Sustained success requires activities that remind you why success matters.

Implement these strategies deliberately. Not all at once—that becomes overwhelming. Pick one or two that feel most relevant. Put them into practice. Notice what helps. Adjust based on experience.

Over time, those small deliberate actions compound into a genuine reconnection with what matters beyond obligations. That reconnection transforms daily experience from constant obligation into a life that includes both responsibilities and genuine engagement with what brings satisfaction.

Start now. Pick one strategy. Take one small action today. Then another tomorrow. That's how lost passion gets reclaimed, not through dramatic transformation, but through accumulated small choices to reconnect with what matters to you.

Chapter 10: Sustaining Your Passion

"Success is not final, failure is not fatal: it is the courage to continue that counts."

—Winston Churchill

Starting something passionate is easier than sustaining it.

Initial excitement provides energy. Novelty creates interest. Early progress feels rewarding. Those first weeks or months, passion feels self-sustaining.

Then reality sets in. The activity becomes familiar. Progress slows. Obstacles appear. Other demands compete for attention. The passionate pursuit that felt effortless initially now requires deliberate effort to maintain.

This is where most passion dies. Not from dramatic failure or loss of interest exactly. Just from gradual deprioritization as initial excitement fades, and sustained effort feels harder to justify.

I've experienced this repeatedly. Started business with intense commitment. That intensity was necessary initially but unsustainable long-term. Had to figure out how to maintain commitment without burning out or letting business become just another obligation.

Same pattern with physical activity, with reading, with any pursuit requiring sustained engagement. Initial enthusiasm carries you briefly. Then you need a different approach to maintain it.

This chapter is about sustaining passion beyond initial excitement. Not through constant intensity, which leads to burnout. But through strategies that make continued engagement feel worthwhile even when it's no longer novel.

Because meaningful achievement requires sustained effort over the years. Initial passion gets you started. Systems and strategies keep you going when initial excitement fades.

Long-Term Motivation

Motivation fluctuates naturally. Some days you feel driven. Other days, you question why you're bothering. That variability is normal, not a sign of failure.

Expecting constant motivation sets you up for disappointment. A better approach is to accept that motivation comes and goes, then build systems that maintain engagement even when motivation is low.

I don't always feel motivated to exercise. Some days, my MS symptoms make movement difficult and unpleasant. But I exercise anyway because I've built it into a routine and I understand the consequences of not doing it.

That's not willpower exactly. It's removing decision-making from the equation. Exercise happens at a scheduled time unless there's a specific reason to skip. Motivation is irrelevant.

Build similar systems for activities you want to sustain. Schedule them. Remove friction between intention and action. Make starting the default rather than something requiring motivation.

But systems alone aren't enough. You also need a connection to why the activity matters beyond immediate experience.

Visualize long-term outcomes regularly. Not wishful fantasizing, but concrete consideration of where sustained effort leads versus where abandoning it leads.

For business, I periodically assess what sustained effort is building versus what would happen if I stopped investing in it. That clarity about stakes helps maintain commitment during periods when daily work feels tedious.

For personal pursuits, consider what sustained engagement provides beyond the activity itself. Physical activity isn't just about immediate workout; it's about maintaining capability as I age with chronic illness. Reading isn't just about an individual book; it's about maintaining perspective and intellectual engagement.

Understanding those broader stakes makes sustained effort feel purposeful even when individual sessions don't feel rewarding.

Set intermediate milestones that provide a sense of progress. Long-term goals feel abstract and distant. Milestones create achievable targets that demonstrate you're making progress.

Celebrate reaching milestones. Not elaborate celebrations necessarily, just acknowledgment that you achieved something. That reinforcement matters for maintaining motivation over time.

I track business metrics monthly. Seeing progress, even small progress, reinforces that consistent effort is producing results. Without that tracking, months of work blend together without a clear sense of advancement.

Surround yourself with people who are also sustaining similar commitments. Their consistent effort normalizes your own. Their struggles remind you that difficulty is normal, not a sign you should quit.

After my diagnosis, I connected with others managing chronic illness while maintaining careers. Seeing them navigate similar challenges made my own struggles feel manageable rather than overwhelming.

Find your equivalent community for whatever you're sustaining. Online groups, local meetups, accountability partners, whatever provides regular contact with others on a similar path.

Mindset affects sustainability enormously. If you believe capabilities are fixed, setbacks feel like evidence you've reached your limit. If you believe capabilities develop through effort, setbacks are just information about what to try next.

That growth mindset, the belief that you can improve through effort, makes sustained engagement feel logical.

You're not trying to maintain passion despite a lack of progress. You're deliberately developing capability through continued practice.

I've improved as a business owner through years of addressing problems I initially didn't know how to solve. That improvement happened because I approached gaps in capability as learnable rather than fixed limitations.

Apply the same thinking to whatever you're sustaining. Current difficulty isn't the ceiling. It's just the current edge of capability. Sustained effort expands that edge.

Connect daily actions to a larger purpose. Why does this activity matter beyond just doing it? What broader goal or value does it serve?

For me, maintaining business serves the purpose of providing for my family and creating value for clients. When daily work feels tedious, connecting it to those purposes restores a sense of meaning.

For personal pursuits, the purpose might be different. Maintaining health so you can do things that matter to you. Developing skill because mastery itself is satisfying. Building community around shared interests.

Whatever the purpose, make it explicit. Remind yourself regularly why you started and why continued effort matters.

Stay flexible about methods while remaining committed to outcomes. The specific way you pursue a goal might need adjusting as circumstances change.

I've modified my business strategy multiple times based on what clients actually needed, rather than what I initially thought they'd want. That flexibility kept the business viable while maintaining the core purpose of helping businesses solve problems.

The same principle applies to personal pursuits. Maybe you can't maintain the exact same practice you started with. Adapt the practice while maintaining core engagement with what matters.

Protect basic maintenance that enables sustained effort. Adequate sleep, reasonable nutrition, some physical activity, and real recovery time. When these basics slip, everything becomes harder, including sustaining passionate pursuits.

I learned this through painful experience. Pushing too hard without adequate recovery created an unsustainable pattern that ultimately reduced performance below what a sustainable pace would have produced.

Build maintenance into the schedule, not something you'll get to when everything else is taken care of. Basic health maintenance is a prerequisite for sustained high performance, not a luxury for when life calms down.

Diversify interests to prevent burnout on any single pursuit. Intense focus on one thing eventually becomes grinding. Having multiple interests provides mental breaks while maintaining overall engagement with meaningful activities.

My business is my primary focus, but it's not my only focus. Reading, physical activity, and time with kids; these other engagements refresh capacity for business work by using different parts of my thinking.

Regularly reassess whether goals still make sense. Circumstances change. You change. What made sense five years ago might not make sense now. That's not failure. It's recognition that sustained effort should serve current reality, not past commitments.

I've modified business goals multiple times based on changing family needs, health considerations, and what I learned about what actually satisfies me professionally.

Be willing to adjust course based on real experience rather than stubbornly maintaining outdated plans.

When motivation dips, and it will, reconnect with what made you care initially. Read material that inspired original interest. Talk to people who share the passion. Revisit early successes that demonstrated why this matters.

That reconnection with origins often restores energy when current experience has become routine.

Practice gratitude for the progress made, rather than just focusing on the distance remaining. It's easy to lose sight of advancement when you're always looking at what's next. Periodically acknowledge how far you've come.

I review annual progress each year. That longer timeframe makes improvement visible that a weekly or monthly assessment might miss. That recognition of actual progress provides motivation that constant future focus doesn't.

Use positive self-talk deliberately. Not delusional optimism, but realistic acknowledgment of your capability and progress. How you talk to yourself about your efforts affects whether those efforts feel worthwhile.

I watch my internal narrative about business challenges. Frame them as problems to solve rather than evidence of inadequacy. That reframing makes sustained effort feel productive rather than futile.

Sustaining long-term motivation isn't about maintaining constant enthusiasm. It's about building systems, connecting to purpose, adapting methods, and employing various strategies to persevere through inevitable periods when immediate motivation is low.

That sustained engagement over the years is what produces meaningful results. Initial passion provides a start. These maintenance strategies provide sustainability.

Adapting to Change

Change disrupts sustained passion more reliably than almost anything else.

You've built routines, developed approaches, and established momentum around a specific way of pursuing what matters. Then circumstances change. Market shifts.

Technology evolves. Your situation changes. Suddenly, your established approaches no longer work as they did.

That disruption challenges sustained passion. You've invested effort in building something that worked. Now you need to adapt, which feels like starting over partially.

I've faced this repeatedly. MS progression changed what physical activities were possible. Client needs have evolved, requiring different service offerings. Technology advancements made old approaches obsolete. Each change required adaptation while maintaining core commitment.

The challenge is adapting methods without losing connection to what you're trying to sustain. Change can either refresh passion by introducing novelty or kill it by making continued effort feel futile.

The difference comes down to how you respond to necessary change.

First: recognize that adaptation isn't failure. It's a response to reality. Circumstances change. Effective approaches change with them. Maintaining the exact same methods regardless of changing context isn't commitment—it's rigidity.

I've had to adapt the business model multiple times. Each adaptation felt uncomfortable initially. But refusal to adapt would have meant business became irrelevant. Adaptation preserved the ability to keep building something I cared about.

The same applies to personal pursuits. Maybe you can't maintain a hobby exactly as you once practiced it. Adapting practice to current circumstances keeps it alive. Refusing to adapt eventually means abandoning it entirely.

Develop a growth mindset about change itself. View changes as opportunities to develop new capabilities rather than threats to established approaches.

When MS forced me to modify physical activities, I initially resented the limitations. Eventually, I reframed it as an opportunity to learn different approaches to maintaining health. That reframing made adaptation feel productive rather than just an accommodation to loss.

Apply similar thinking to changes affecting your sustained passions. What can you learn from necessary adaptation? How might new approaches offer advantages that old methods didn't?

Stay informed about developments in fields that matter to you. Change is less disruptive when you see it coming and can adapt proactively rather than reactively.

I stay informed about industry trends, technological developments, and economic shifts that are relevant to my business. That awareness allows me to adjust my strategy before a change becomes a crisis.

Same principle for personal pursuits. Stay current with developments in areas you care about. That ongoing learning helps you adapt smoothly rather than being blindsided by change.

Build flexibility into your approach to pursuing goals. Don't become so attached to specific methods that you can't adjust when circumstances require it.

I'm committed to helping businesses solve problems. But I'm flexible about what services require, how those services get delivered, and what industries I work with. That flexibility allowed me to adapt to changing market needs while maintaining my core purpose.

Identify what's essential versus what's just familiar. Essential elements need to be protected during change. Familiar elements that aren't actually essential can be modified without losing what matters.

For me, business success requires delivering genuine value to clients. The specific services, delivery methods, and pricing structures are all adaptable. As long as I'm solving real problems effectively, the business serves its purpose regardless of specific form.

Make a similar distinction for your pursuits. What's the essential core that makes this matter to you? What's just the current expression of that core? Protecting the core while adapting expression enables change without loss.

Leverage the community during adaptation periods. Others pursuing similar passions have likely faced similar changes. Learning from their adaptations saves you from reinventing solutions.

When I needed to modify physical activities due to MS, I connected with others managing similar health challenges.

Their experience adapting exercise routines provided practical approaches I wouldn't have discovered alone.

Find your equivalent resources. Who's navigated the changes you're facing? What can you learn from their adaptations?

Embrace useful technology and tools even if they require learning new approaches. Technology often enables capabilities that weren't possible with old methods.

I've adopted new business tools multiple times. Each required a learning curve. But each also enabled efficiencies or capabilities that improved what I could deliver. That improvement justified the adaptation effort.

Don't resist technology just because it's different from familiar methods. Evaluate whether it enables better pursuit of what matters.

Maintain self-care, especially during periods of change. Adaptation requires mental and physical capacity. If you're depleted, even necessary change feels overwhelming.

During major business transitions, I deliberately protected sleep, exercise, and recovery time. That maintenance provided the capacity to handle adaptation demands without burning out.

Treat change periods as requiring extra maintenance, not as justification for abandoning them.

Celebrate successful adaptations. Each time you navigate change without losing core commitment, acknowledge that achievement. It builds confidence for handling future changes.

I track major business adaptations and their outcomes. Reviewing those successful transitions reminds me that I can handle change when the next one appears.

Build a similar record for yourself. Evidence of past successful adaptation makes future change feel manageable.

Understand that passion evolves. What you care about and how you pursue it naturally change as you develop. That evolution is healthy, not deterioration.

My business focus has shifted multiple times based on what I learned about what problems I solve best and what work I find most satisfying. Those shifts represented evolution, not abandonment of the original vision.

Allow your passions to evolve. The core might remain consistent while expression changes significantly. That's growth, not loss of commitment.

When change feels overwhelming, break adaptation into smaller steps. You don't need to completely reinvent the approach immediately. Small adjustments accumulate into major adaptations.

I've never completely overhauled business strategy at once. Each major change happened through a series of smaller adjustments, each manageable individually.

Use the same incremental approach for the adaptations you're facing. What's one small adjustment you can make now? Then another? That progression feels doable in ways that complete reinvention doesn't.

Remember that temporary disruption during adaptation is normal. Performance often dips while you're learning new approaches. That's not failure. It's a natural part of the transition.

Every time I've modified my business model, there's been an awkward period while figuring out the new approach. But that temporary dip was a necessary price for longer-term improvement.

Expect similar patterns in your adaptations. Temporary difficulty doesn't mean the change was wrong. It means you're learning.

View change as inevitable rather than exceptional. Circumstances always change. Effective pursuit of anything meaningful requires ongoing adaptation as a normal part of the process, not crisis management.

That expectation of change makes it feel like part of the journey rather than a disaster interrupting it. You're not trying to maintain a fixed approach forever. You're sustaining core commitment while continuously adapting expression.

That combination: committed core, flexible methods, creates sustainability that rigid approaches never achieve. The core provides direction and meaning. Flexibility enables continued relevance as circumstances evolve.

Build both. Clarity about what matters enough to sustain long-term. Flexibility about how you sustain it as conditions change. That combination creates passion that endures through inevitable changes rather than being destroyed by them.

Chapter 11: Strategies for Staying Motivated

"It's not that I'm so smart, it's just that I stay with problems longer."

—Albert Einstein

Motivation fluctuates. That's not a character flaw or a sign you're doing something wrong. It's a normal human experience.

Some days you wake up energized and ready to tackle challenges. Other days, getting started feels like pushing a boulder uphill. That variability is part of being human, not evidence of inadequacy.

The mistake people make is assuming sustained effort requires sustained motivation. When motivation inevitably dips, they often conclude that they've lost passion for what they're doing or that they're not suited for it.

That's backwards. Sustained effort comes from systems and strategies that work regardless of motivation levels, not from maintaining constant enthusiasm.

After my MS diagnosis, I couldn't rely on motivation. Some days, my symptoms made everything harder. Energy was limited. Mental clarity fluctuated. If I'd waited for motivation to show up, nothing would have gotten done.

Had to build approaches that maintained progress even when motivation was low or completely absent. Those strategies became the foundation for building a business and managing life despite unpredictable health challenges.

This chapter is about practical strategies for maintaining effort when motivation is low, not through manufactured enthusiasm or positive thinking, but through concrete approaches that work when you don't feel like working.

Because meaningful achievement requires sustained effort over the years, motivation provides occasional boosts. Systems and strategies provide sustainability between those boosts.

Setbacks destroy motivation more reliably than almost anything else.

You're working toward your goal, making progress, and feeling reasonably good about your trajectory. Then something goes wrong. Client leaves. Project fails. Illness flares. Relationship ends. Whatever the specific setback, it undermines the sense of progress and raises questions about whether continued effort is worthwhile.

That's when most people quit. Not during initial enthusiasm when everything feels possible, but after a setback that makes the path feel blocked.

I've faced this repeatedly. Business clients who left despite good work. Service offerings that attracted no interest. Marketing efforts that generated zero response. Health setbacks that disrupted everything.

Each one felt like evidence that maybe this wasn't going to work. Maybe I should quit and try something else. Maybe I was fooling myself thinking I could build a sustainable business while managing chronic illness.

But quitting after every setback would mean never accomplishing anything because setbacks are inevitable in any worthwhile pursuit. They're not signs you're on the wrong path; they're just part of any path.

The question isn't whether you'll face setbacks. It's how you respond when they occur.

First: recognize that a setback doesn't mean total failure. It means that a specific approach didn't work or a specific circumstance didn't go as hoped. That's information, not a verdict on the entire pursuit.

When a client leaves, it doesn't mean my business is failing. It means that the particular client relationship didn't work out. Maybe I wasn't the right fit for their needs. Maybe their needs changed. Maybe I made mistakes in that relationship.

Any of those possibilities provides information about what to do differently going forward. None of them means I should abandon the entire business.

Train yourself to ask "what does this specific setback tell me?" rather than "does this setback mean I should quit?"

Second: distinguish between setbacks that require a strategy change versus setbacks that just require persistence through difficulty.

Some setbacks reveal fundamental problems with the approach. If you've tried the same strategy repeatedly with consistently poor results, that's a signal to try a different approach.

Other setbacks are just normal friction and variability. One failed attempt doesn't mean the approach is wrong. It might just mean this particular instance didn't work out.

I've learned to assess whether a setback represents a pattern requiring strategic change or just normal variability. That distinction prevents both giving up too quickly and persisting with broken approaches too long.

Third: use setbacks to identify actual problems rather than just feeling discouraged.

When something goes wrong, resist the initial emotional reaction to just feel bad about it. Instead, analyze what actually happened and why.

Client left... why? Was there misalignment in expectations? Did I fail to deliver what I promised? Did their needs change in ways I didn't anticipate?

Understanding the actual cause provides direction for improvement. Just feeling discouraged provides nothing useful.

I keep brief notes on what went wrong in setbacks. That documentation helps identify patterns; the same problems appearing repeatedly signal issues needing systematic solutions rather than just bad luck.

Fourth: maintain perspective on what setbacks actually cost versus what they feel like they cost.

A failed project feels like a massive emotional failure. But objectively, what did it actually cost? Sometimes an effort didn't produce the intended results. That's disappointing, but it's not catastrophic.

The lost client feels like the evidence business is collapsing. But objectively, it's one relationship ending. I still have other clients. Business continues operating.

That logical assessment of actual impact helps separate emotional reaction from practical reality. The emotional reaction is valid; setbacks feel bad. But the practical impact is often much less severe than it feels.

Fifth: lean on a support network during setbacks instead of isolating.

The natural tendency after a setback is to withdraw and deal with it alone. That isolation makes everything worse because you're left with only your own discouragement for perspective.

Other people provide different perspectives. They might see solutions you're missing. They remind you that one setback doesn't define the entire trajectory. They've faced similar setbacks and can share how they navigated them.

I deliberately reach out to business owner friends when facing setbacks. Their outside perspective helps me assess the situation more accurately than I can alone, even when I'm discouraged.

Build relationships before you need them so support is available when setbacks occur.

Sixth: Reconnect with why you started when setbacks make you question whether to continue.

In the immediate aftermath of a setback, it's easy to forget why you cared about this pursuit initially. The current difficulty feels more real than the original purpose.

Deliberately reconnect with original motivation. Not to manufacture false enthusiasm, but to assess whether the underlying purpose still matters despite the current setback.

For me, the original purpose was to provide for my family while building a business I was proud of. That purpose remains valid even when specific clients leave or approaches fail.

If the underlying purpose still matters, continue despite a setback. If the purpose no longer resonates, then maybe it is time to change direction. But make that decision based on purpose, not just current discouragement.

Seventh: use setbacks to build resilience rather than seeing them only as obstacles.

Each setback you navigate successfully increases confidence that you can handle future setbacks. That accumulated resilience makes subsequent difficulties more manageable.

I've handled enough business setbacks now that new ones feel less devastating. I know from experience I can adapt and continue despite difficulty. That knowledge came from actually navigating previous setbacks, not from avoiding them.

View setbacks as building resilience for future challenges rather than only as current problems. That reframing doesn't eliminate difficulty but makes it feel productive rather than purely negative.

Eighth: maintain basic self-care during setbacks instead of abandoning it when stressed.

When things go wrong, the tendency is either to push harder while neglecting health or to give up on everything, including maintenance. Both approaches make setbacks harder to navigate.

Continue exercise, adequate sleep, and reasonable nutrition even during difficult periods. That maintenance provides the capacity to handle challenges. Abandoning it when stressed eliminates resources when you need them most.

I protect basic health maintenance, especially during difficult periods. That consistency helps me navigate challenges with whatever capability I have, rather than letting everything deteriorate together.

Setbacks are inevitable. Your response to them determines whether they end your efforts or just temporarily slow progress, which you can resume afterward.

Build these response strategies before you need them. Practice seeing setbacks as information rather than verdicts. Maintain support networks. Protect basic self-care. Reconnect with purpose when difficulty makes you question continuation.

Those strategies won't eliminate setbacks or make them pleasant. But they'll help you navigate them without quitting every time things get difficult.

Maintaining focus on long-term goals while managing daily demands is harder than it sounds.

Goals set during motivated moments feel compelling. You're clear about what you want to achieve and why it matters. That clarity creates initial momentum.

Then daily reality intervenes. Immediate demands consume attention. Urgent issues require responses. Long-term goals that seemed important during the planning session get pushed aside by today's crisis or opportunity.

Months pass. You realize you've been busy but haven't made meaningful progress on goals that supposedly mattered. Not because you decided they didn't matter, but because daily urgency consistently displaced them.

I've experienced this repeatedly. Set quarterly business goals during reflection periods when I have perspective. Then, daily client work and immediate operational issues consume actual time. Quarter ends with goals barely addressed despite genuine intention.

Had to develop strategies that maintain focus on longer-term goals despite the daily urgency that naturally dominates attention.

First: translate abstract goals into concrete next actions.

"Grow business" is the goal. But it's too abstract to act on directly. What specific action moves toward that goal this week?

For me, it might involve: reaching out to three potential clients, completing a case study documenting recent success, and improving one specific service offering based on client feedback.

Those concrete actions connect to a broader goal but are specific enough to actually do. Abstract goals stay abstract. Concrete actions create progress.

What next action moves toward your goal this week? Schedule it. Actually do it. That's how abstract goals become real progress.

Second: protect a specific time for goal-related work instead of fitting it into whatever time remains after urgent matters.

If goal-work only happens when there's extra time after urgent matters are handled, it rarely happens. There's always another urgent matter.

Schedule goal-work time like you'd schedule an important meeting. Treat it as committed time, not available time that urgent matters can claim.

I block mornings for strategic work on business development and improvement. Client work and operational urgencies happen in the afternoons. That boundary ensures that goals are addressed regularly, rather than only when everything else is taken care of.

What time could you protect for goal-related work? Not aspirational "I'll find time," but specific, scheduled, protected time?

Third: break large goals into smaller milestones that provide a sense of progress.

A year-long goal is too distant to motivate daily action. You need intermediate targets that demonstrate progress and create momentum.

My annual business goals break into quarterly milestones and monthly targets. Those intermediate points make progress visible and create regular opportunities to celebrate advancement, rather than just seeing the distance remaining.

What milestones between the current state and the eventual goal would make progress visible? Schedule them. Track them. Acknowledge when you reach them.

Fourth: Build goal-related activities into your routine instead of treating them as separate projects that require motivation.

If pursuing a goal requires special motivation to take action, you'll only make progress when motivated. Build goal work into a regular routine, so it happens regardless of your motivational state.

I write daily as part of a routine, not a special project requiring inspiration. Some days writing goes well. Other days it's difficult. But it happens regardless because it's a scheduled routine, not a motivation-dependent activity.

What goal-related activity could become routine rather than a motivation-dependent project? Schedule it as a regular practice.

Fifth: minimize context-switching that fragments attention.

Constantly shifting between different types of work prevents deep focus on any of them. Goal work, especially, suffers because it typically requires deeper thinking than urgent operational tasks.

Batch similar activities together. Do all similar tasks in one session rather than switching constantly. That reduces transition costs and enables better focus during each work session.

I handle all client communications in specific periods rather than constantly throughout the day. That batching prevents communication from fragmenting focus during strategic work periods.

What batching would reduce your context-switching? Group similar activities together instead of mixing them throughout the day.

Sixth: regularly reassess whether goals still align with actual priorities.

Sometimes, a lack of progress on a goal reveals that the goal doesn't actually matter as much as you thought when you set it. Rather than forcing effort toward a goal that doesn't truly motivate you, reassess whether it still deserves pursuit.

I review quarterly whether current goals still serve the purposes I care about. Some goals persist. Others get modified or abandoned as understanding evolves about what actually matters.

That willingness to adjust goals prevents wasting effort on outdated objectives that no longer serve current priorities.

Seventh: limit commitments to protect capacity for goal-work.

Every commitment consumes time and energy. Too many commitments mean no capacity remains for goal-related work, regardless of intentions.

Learn to decline requests that don't serve important priorities. That selectivity creates space for work that does matter.

I've become more selective about which opportunities and requests I accept. Not refusing everything, just being more deliberate about which commitments serve important goals.

Where could you be more selective to protect capacity for goal-work?

Eighth: Use accountability structures that create external pressure when internal motivation is low.

Telling others about goals creates mild accountability. Regular check-ins with an accountability partner or group create stronger accountability. Public commitment creates the strongest accountability.

That external pressure helps maintain effort when internal motivation dips.

I have regular check-ins with the business owner peer group. Knowing I'll report progress helps maintain effort during weeks when motivation is low.

What accountability structure would help you maintain focus? Find an accountability partner, join a group, make a public commitment, or whatever provides helpful external pressure.

Ninth: track progress visibly so advancement is apparent instead of just seeing distance remaining.

Looking only at how far you still need to go creates discouragement. Tracking progress made creates momentum and demonstrates that effort is producing results.

I track monthly business metrics and quarterly progress toward annual goals. That visible tracking shows an advancement that maintaining only future focus would miss.

How could you make progress visible? Create a tracking system that shows advancement, not just distance to destination.

Remember that focus doesn't mean constant attention to goals while ignoring everything else. It means ensuring that goals receive regular attention, despite the daily urgencies that naturally dominate awareness.

Build these focus strategies into regular practice. Schedule goal-work time. Break goals into milestones. Create accountability. Track progress. Reassess periodically.

That systematic approach maintains progress on long-term goals despite short-term urgencies that would otherwise consume all available attention and energy.

Chapter 12: Reviewing Progress

"Without reflection, we go blindly on our way, creating more unintended consequences and failing to achieve anything useful."

—Margaret J. Wheatley

Most people rarely assess whether their efforts are actually producing desired results.

They work consistently, stay busy, and complete tasks. But they don't systematically evaluate whether that activity is moving them toward goals that matter or just consuming time without meaningful progress.

Without regular assessment, you can spend years working hard on things that don't actually serve your priorities. Busy but not effective. Active but not advancing.

I've fallen into this pattern repeatedly. Get absorbed in daily client work, operational tasks, and immediate demands. Months pass before I realize I've been busy but haven't made progress on goals I claimed were priorities.

That realization is uncomfortable. I've been working hard. Where did the effort go? Why don't results match intentions?

The problem isn't insufficient effort. It's a lack of systematic review connecting effort to outcomes. Without regular assessment, daily urgency dominates while important non-urgent goals get perpetually deferred.

Had to build review practices that force honest evaluation of whether actions align with stated priorities and whether those actions produce intended results.

This chapter is about systematic progress review. Not just acknowledging what you accomplished, but honestly assessing whether accomplishments serve purposes you actually care about. About using that assessment to adjust the approach rather than just continuing whatever you're currently doing.

Measuring progress requires clarity about what you're trying to achieve and why.

Sounds obvious. But many people pursue goals without clearly defining what success actually looks like. "Grow business," or "get healthier," or "be more successful"—these aspirations don't provide concrete targets enabling assessment of whether you're making progress.

Without a clear definition of success, you can't measure whether you're achieving it. You're left with a vague sense of whether things feel like they're going well, which is an unreliable guide.

The first step is defining what success actually means for the goals you're pursuing. Not abstract ideals, but concrete outcomes you could objectively assess.

For my business, success means having sufficient revenue to support my family, working on projects I'm proud of with clients I respect, maintaining a sustainable workload despite health constraints, and continuing to learn and develop in areas I care about.

Those criteria are specific enough that I can assess whether I'm achieving them. Revenue is measurable. Whether I'm proud of my work is subjective, but it can be assessed through reflection. Sustainability is evident in whether I'm able to maintain effort without constant crisis.

What does success actually mean for your priorities? Be specific enough that you could honestly assess whether you're achieving it.

Distinguish between output metrics and outcome metrics. Output is what you do. Outcome is what results from what you do. They're not the same.

Output: hours worked, tasks completed, activities performed. Outcome: revenue generated, problems solved, value created, capabilities developed.

It's possible to have impressive output metrics: worked many hours, completed many tasks, while achieving poor outcomes. The work didn't produce the intended results despite consuming significant effort.

Focus assessment primarily on outcomes, not just outputs. Are you achieving results that matter, not just staying busy?

For my business, output would be measured in hours billed or the number of client meetings. The outcome is whether clients' problems were actually solved and whether they value the work enough to continue engaging.

High output with poor outcomes means I'm working hard on the wrong things. That's valuable information requiring strategic adjustment.

What outcomes actually matter for your priorities? How will you assess whether you're achieving them?

Some important outcomes aren't easily quantified. Quality of relationships. Sense of meaning in work. Personal development and growth. These matter but resist simple measurement.

For qualitative outcomes, use reflective assessment instead of metrics. Regular journaling or reflection sessions where you honestly assess: Is this aspect improving, staying steady, or declining?

I assess quarterly whether work still feels meaningful, whether I'm developing capabilities I care about, and whether relationships with important people are strong or deteriorating.

Can't reduce these to numbers. But can honestly assess trajectory through reflection.

Build a regular review cadence rather than only assessing when something feels wrong. Monthly or quarterly reviews work well for most people. Frequency matters less than consistency.

I review monthly for operational metrics and quarterly for strategic assessment. That rhythm catches problems before they become crises and identifies opportunities while they're still relevant.

What review frequency makes sense for your situation? Schedule it. Actually do it consistently.

During reviews, assess both what's working and what isn't. The natural tendency is to focus only on problems that need fixing. But understanding what's working helps you do more of it.

When I review business performance, I note what produced good results as well as what didn't work. Often patterns emerge, certain types of work consistently satisfy both my clients and me, while other types consistently create problems.

That information guides strategy: do more of what works, less of what doesn't. Sounds obvious, but requires systematic assessment to identify patterns.

Compare actual results to intentions from the previous review. Did you accomplish what you intended? If not, why not?

Sometimes the gap between intention and results reveals unrealistic planning. Sometimes it reveals that priority wasn't actually as important as you thought when you set it. Sometimes it reveals obstacles that need addressing.

Understanding why intentions didn't translate to results provides direction for adjustment.

I frequently find that goals I set weren't achieved because they weren't actually priorities, despite my claims. Other activities consistently displaced them. That reveals either a need to protect time for those goals or a need to acknowledge they're not actually priorities and stop claiming they are.

That honest assessment prevents continuing to feel bad about not achieving goals I'm not actually committed to pursuing.

Be willing to adjust goals based on what the review reveals. Sometimes, a lack of progress indicates the need for a different approach. Sometimes it indicates the goal itself needs reconsidering.

I've abandoned business goals after a quarterly review revealed they no longer served the purposes I cared about. That wasn't a failure; it was a course correction based on an evolved understanding.

Use metrics and assessment as tools for learning, not just scorekeeping. The point isn't proving you're succeeding or failing. It's understanding what's actually happening so you can adjust your approach.

That learning orientation makes review valuable even when results are disappointing. Poor results paired with honest assessment provide direction for improvement. Poor results without assessment just feel discouraging.

Track progress visibly so advancement is apparent. Easy to only see the distance remaining toward the eventual goal. Visible tracking of progress made provides balance by showing advancement even when the destination is still distant.

I maintain simple tracking of key business metrics and quarterly progress toward annual goals. When the current week feels difficult, reviewing accumulated progress over months provides perspective that immediate frustration doesn't.

How could you make progress visible rather than only focusing on the gap between the current state and the eventual goal?

Remember that the purpose of the review is to inform adjustment, not to judge adequacy. You're not trying to prove you're good enough. You're trying to understand what's working so you can do more of it and what isn't working so you can change your approach.

That pragmatic orientation makes the review useful rather than just an uncomfortable self-judgment exercise.

Progress toward significant goals happens gradually through accumulated small advancements.

The problem is that small daily progress doesn't feel significant while it's happening. You're working consistently, but any individual day's contribution feels minimal. Over the course of months, that work compounds into meaningful progress, but during the daily grind, it's hard to feel like you're accomplishing anything.

That lack of felt progress undermines motivation. When effort doesn't feel like it's producing results, continuing becomes harder. You question whether sustained effort is worthwhile.

Celebrating milestones addresses this by creating regular acknowledgment of progress that daily experience doesn't provide naturally.

A milestone is an intermediate target between the starting point and the eventual goal. Achievement is substantial enough to feel meaningful but occurring frequently enough to provide regular reinforcement.

For a year-long goal, quarterly milestones work well. For a multi-year goal, annual milestones. For smaller goals, monthly milestones might make sense.

The key is frequency matching the goal timeframe, so you're regularly acknowledging progress rather than only celebrating final achievement after years of effort.

I set quarterly business milestones for annual goals. Reaching those milestones provides regular reinforcement that effort is producing progress, even though the eventual goal remains distant.

What milestone frequency makes sense for your goals? Not so frequent that they feel trivial, but frequent enough to provide regular acknowledgment of progress.

Celebration doesn't require elaborate events. It requires a deliberate acknowledgment that a milestone has been reached and that achievement matters.

It might be a brief reflection on the progress. You might be sharing your achievement with people who care about your success. It might be a small personal reward, such as dinner out or an afternoon off, whatever feels celebratory to you.

The specific form matters less than deliberate acknowledgment. You're making progress rather than immediately moving to the next target without recognizing the advancement.

I note milestone achievements in monthly reviews and share them with the business peer group. That acknowledgment, both private reflection and social sharing, makes progress feel real rather than just a continued grind toward a distant goal.

How will you mark milestone achievements? Make it concrete rather than a vague intention to "celebrate somehow."

Celebration serves multiple functions beyond just feeling good momentarily.

First, it reinforces that sustained effort produces results. Your brain learns patterns:

Consistent work → Progress → Acknowledgment

That reinforcement makes continued effort feel worthwhile.

Second, it creates concrete evidence of capability. When facing a new challenge, you can recall previous milestones achieved. That evidence counters doubt about whether you can handle the current difficulty.

Third, it maintains morale during the difficult middle periods between the initial enthusiasm and eventual completion. Those middle periods are when most people quit; the initial excitement has faded, and the destination remains distant. Milestones provide reinforcement that sustains effort through that vulnerable period.

I use past milestone achievements as evidence when facing new challenges. I've solved similar problems before. I've maintained effort through difficult periods before. Historical evidence supports continuing through current difficulties.

Small wins deserve acknowledgment even though they're not major milestones. Completed a difficult task. Solved the persistent problem. Maintained commitment during a challenging week.

These small wins are building blocks creating larger progress. Acknowledging them reinforces the daily effort that eventually produces milestone achievements.

I note weekly what went well alongside identifying what needs improvement. That practice of acknowledging small wins prevents perspective from becoming only a catalog of problems and gaps.

What small wins from this week deserve acknowledgment?

Be specific about what you're celebrating. Not just "made progress," but what specifically advanced and why that matters.

"Completed three client projects this month" is concrete. Understanding why that matters—demonstrated reliable delivery, generated revenue, built client relationships—connects achievement to purposes you care about.

That specificity makes celebration meaningful rather than just going through motions of acknowledging something happened.

Share milestone achievements with people who care about your success. That social acknowledgment makes progress feel more real and strengthens relationships with people supporting your efforts.

I share quarterly business progress with my mentor, business peer group, and family. Their acknowledgment and celebration amplify my own recognition of progress.

Who would genuinely care about your milestone achievements? Share them rather than only privately noting progress.

Use visual representations of progress. Charts showing advancement. Lists of completed milestones. Whatever makes accumulated progress visible rather than just existing in memory.

I maintain simple visual tracking of progress toward annual goals. When motivation dips, reviewing a visible representation of progress made over months provides concrete evidence that effort is producing results.

What visual representation would make your progress apparent?

Acknowledge collective achievements when progress involved others. Team completed project. Collaboration produced results. The community achieved its shared goal.

That shared celebration strengthens relationships and reinforces that meaningful achievement often involves multiple people contributing toward a common purpose.

For my business, I acknowledge that progress has resulted from good client relationships, helpful peer advice, or family support, enabling me to focus on my work. That recognition reinforces those relationships while celebrating achievement.

Be honest about what milestones actually represent. Reaching a milestone is meaningful progress, but it's not completion. Celebration acknowledges advancement while recognizing that work continues.

That balance, celebrating progress without treating milestones as an endpoint, maintains momentum forward while providing reinforcement for effort already invested.

I celebrate quarterly milestones while acknowledging they're steps toward larger annual goals. That framing makes celebration meaningful without implying work is finished.

Use the milestone celebration as an opportunity for brief reflection. What enabled reaching this milestone? What should continue? What should be adjusted going forward?

That reflection converts celebration into a learning opportunity, making it useful beyond just momentary acknowledgment.

Remember that milestone frequency and celebration style should match your personality and situation. Some people need frequent acknowledgment. Others find that excessive and prefer less frequent but more substantial celebrations.

Experiment with what actually helps maintain your motivation. Adjust based on experience rather than following someone else's formula.

The goal is to create regular reinforcement that shows sustained effort produces meaningful progress. However, the approach you take, through your chosen milestone frequency and celebration style, is the right one for you.

Build this practice deliberately. Set milestones. Actually acknowledge when you reach them. Use that acknowledgment to maintain motivation through the extended effort required for meaningful achievement.

That systematic celebration converts a long, difficult journey into a series of acknowledged steps, making sustained effort feel worthwhile rather than an endless grind toward a distant goal.

Chapter 13: The Ultimate Power of Passion

"The only way to do great work is to love what you do."

—Steve Jobs

We've covered substantial ground exploring passion from multiple angles throughout this book.

What it actually means beyond motivational platitudes. How to identify what genuinely matters to you. Obstacles that undermine passionate pursuit. Strategies for maintaining engagement over the years. Ways to integrate passion into daily life despite competing demands.

Now the question becomes: what does this all add up to? What actually becomes possible when you build life around what you care about rather than just pursuing conventional success markers?

This isn't a theoretical question for me. I've lived both approaches. Early in my career, I pursued opportunities that seemed like smart moves for advancement. Made decent progress. Earned a reasonable income. Checked expected boxes.

But something fundamental was missing. The work didn't engage me beyond earning a paycheck. Success by external measures didn't create internal satisfaction. I was functioning but not fulfilled.

After my MS diagnosis forced reevaluation of everything, I rebuilt around what actually mattered to me. Work I was proud of with clients I respected. Time with family that felt connected. Maintaining the capability to do things I cared about. Contributing to the community of other entrepreneurs.

That shift, from pursuing what seemed successful to pursuing what actually mattered, changed everything. Not magically. Not without continued difficulty. But fundamentally.

This final chapter explores what becomes possible when you actually apply these principles consistently over time. The real power of passion isn't mystical. It's a practical advantage that compounds when you align sustained effort with genuine interest and purpose.

"Unstoppable success" sounds like motivational hype. But there's a real phenomenon worth understanding.

When you're pursuing what genuinely matters to you, not what sounds impressive or what others expect, you develop a different relationship with obstacles and setbacks.

Difficulties don't stop feeling difficult. Setbacks still create frustration. Obstacles still require real effort to overcome. The challenges don't disappear just because you care about what you're doing.

What changes is your response to difficulty.

When you're pursuing something because you think you should or because it seems like a path to success, setbacks raise an immediate question: Is this worth it? Should I quit and try something else?

When you're pursuing something you genuinely care about, that question still appears during difficult periods. But the answer is different. The difficulty doesn't make you question whether to continue. It prompts you to question what needs to change to continue effectively.

I experienced this contrast directly. Early career, pursuing opportunities that seemed like smart moves, when they became difficult, and everything becomes difficult eventually, I questioned whether to persist. Had no deep reason to continue beyond abstract career advancement.

Building a business around work I actually care about, difficulty still appears constantly. Client challenges. Health setbacks. Operational problems. Market changes require adaptation. Each creates real frustration and requires significant effort.

But I don't question whether to continue the business. I question how to continue effectively given current constraints. That shift, from whether to continue to how to continue, is what makes the effort "unstoppable."

Not because obstacles don't exist. But because obstacles don't trigger abandonment consideration. They trigger problem-solving instead.

That persistence through difficulty is what eventually produces significant achievement. Not because passionate people are superhuman. Because they keep working through periods when people pursuing less meaningful goals quit.

Most people abandon pursuits during difficult middle periods. Initial enthusiasm fades. Destination still distant. Progress feels slow. Obstacles accumulate. That's when most efforts die, not from dramatic failure, but from gradual abandonment as difficulty makes continuation feel not worthwhile.

Passion doesn't eliminate those difficult middle periods. However, it alters the calculation about whether to continue. When work matters beyond just outcomes, continuing through difficulty feels logical despite frustration.

That persistence eventually produces results that shorter-term efforts never achieve. Not because passionate people are more talented. Because they stay engaged long enough for compounded effort to produce significant outcomes.

This is mechanical, not mystical. Sustained effort over the years produces results that sporadic effort never does. Passion enables that sustained effort by making continuation feel worthwhile despite difficulty.

But, and this matters enormously, passion alone isn't sufficient.

Passionate pursuit of misguided goals just means you'll persist at something ineffective. Passion without strategy means sustained effort in the wrong direction. Enthusiasm without discipline becomes exhausting intensity that burns out.

The power comes from combining passion with strategic thinking and disciplined execution.

I'm passionate about my business. But that passion would be useless without understanding how to actually serve clients effectively, manage operations sustainably, adapt to market changes, and maintain financial viability.

The passion provides motivation to continue developing those capabilities. The capabilities actually produce results. Both matter. Neither alone is sufficient.

So when building toward "unstoppable success," start with what you actually care about. But then apply rigorous strategic thinking. What capabilities do you need? What resources? What approach makes sense given actual constraints? What needs learning or developing?

That combination, genuine care about outcomes plus strategic capability, creates unstoppable momentum. Not because you never face obstacles. Because obstacles don't stop you. They just require solving.

Write down what you're actually trying to achieve and why it matters to you personally. Not what sounds impressive. What you actually care about, regardless of whether others would be impressed.

Then, honestly assess what capability-building is required. What do you need to learn? What resources need developing? What relationships need building? What approaches need testing?

Develop a strategic plan that connects passionate purpose to the concrete development of capabilities needed. Then execute that plan persistently while learning from results and adapting the approach.

That's the formula for unstoppable success. Clear about what matters. Strategic about building capability. Persistent through difficulty because the purpose sustains effort. Adaptive because learning improves the approach.

Not magical. But reliably effective when applied consistently over time.

Surround yourself with people pursuing similar approaches. Their example normalizes persistence through difficulty. Their experience provides perspective during your challenging periods. Their success demonstrates what's possible through sustained effort.

I've built a network of other entrepreneurs managing health challenges while building businesses. That community provides both practical support and proof that my goals are achievable despite constraints.

Find your equivalent community. Who's doing what you're attempting? How can you build relationships with them?

Celebrate progress milestones along the way. Major achievements take years. If you only acknowledge completion, you'll spend years without reinforcement. Regular milestone celebration maintains motivation through extended effort.

I celebrate quarterly progress toward annual goals. Those regular acknowledgments provide reinforcement that effort is producing results even when the eventual destination remains distant.

Balance intensity with sustainability. Passion can drive destructive overwork as easily as productive effort. Build a sustainable pace you can maintain for years, not a maximum intensity you can't sustain.

I learned this through burnout. Pushing too hard because I cared about work created an unsustainable pattern that ultimately reduced effectiveness below what a sustainable effort would have produced.

Protect health maintenance, relationships, and restoration activities even while pursuing passionate goals. Those aren't obstacles to success. They're foundations that enable sustained high performance over the years.

Remember that unstoppable success isn't avoiding difficulty. It's persisting through difficulty because what you're pursuing matters enough to make continued effort feel worthwhile despite challenges.

Build that foundation deliberately. Clarify what actually matters to you. Develop the capabilities required. Persist through difficulty. Learn and adapt continuously. Maintain sustainability. Celebrate progress.

That approach creates momentum that compounds over the years into outcomes that seem impossible to people who don't understand the power of sustained passionate effort.

Passion isn't just useful for achieving specific goals. It's a foundation for life that feels worth living regardless of particular achievements.

Most people experience passion most intensely during youth. Children and teenagers engage enthusiastically with interests before adult responsibilities and practical concerns crowd out activities done purely because they matter.

Then adulthood arrives with its demands. Career building. Financial responsibilities. Family obligations. Health management. The activities that once engaged you deeply get pushed aside as luxuries you'll return to "someday when life calms down."

Except life doesn't calm down. The demands just shift. If you're waiting for perfect conditions to reconnect with what matters, you'll wait indefinitely.

I experienced this directly. Before my MS diagnosis, I'd gradually abandoned most activities I did just because I enjoyed them. Everything became utilitarian: advance one's career, earn an income, and meet obligations. No space remained for activities done purely because they interested me.

After diagnosis, facing the prospect of declining capability, I realized I couldn't keep deferring engagement with what actually mattered. Had to rebuild it deliberately, despite constraints, rather than waiting for them to disappear.

That reconnection wasn't returning to the exact activities I'd enjoyed earlier. Circumstances had changed. My interests had evolved. Physical limitations prevented some previous activities.

But the core pattern remained, making space for activities I cared about beyond just their utility. Reading for interest, not just professional development. Time with kids that felt connected, not just managing them. Physical activity for capability maintenance, not just an exercise obligation.

That shift restored something essential that the gradual abandonment of passion had eliminated. Life felt worth living again, rather than just a series of obligations to complete.

A lifelong passion isn't about maintaining identical interests forever. It's a sustaining practice of engaging with what matters to you throughout life, despite changing circumstances and evolving interests.

The specific interests may shift. What mattered at twenty might not matter at forty. That evolution is healthy. But the pattern of making space for what matters beyond utility, that pattern needs to be maintained throughout life.

Many people hit a midlife crisis when they realize they've built a successful life by external measures that doesn't feel satisfying internally. Good career, adequate income, stable family—all the boxes checked. But something fundamental is missing.

That missing element is usually passion. They've spent decades pursuing what seemed sensible while gradually abandoning what actually mattered to them. The success feels hollow because it's disconnected from genuine interests and values.

Reconnecting with passion during those periods transforms experience dramatically. Not necessarily through radical life changes, though sometimes that's appropriate. But through deliberately creating space for what matters even within existing constraints.

Small, consistent engagement with what you care about transforms daily experience. Fifteen minutes daily reading what interests you. Weekly time on a hobby you enjoy. Regular connection with the community, sharing your interests. These modest investments restore elements that purely functional existence eliminates.

For me, protecting morning reading time and staying connected with the business owner community maintains engagement beyond just completing daily obligations. Those small, consistent practices keep life feeling meaningful rather than just busy.

What activities connect you to what matters beyond utility? What interests have you abandoned that deserve reclaiming? What communities align with values you care about?

Start rebuilding the connection deliberately. Not through a dramatic overhaul necessarily. Through small sustainable practices that maintain engagement despite competing demands.

Professional life benefits enormously from sustained passion. People passionate about their work bring energy and innovation that people just doing jobs for income can't match.

Clients and colleagues notice genuine engagement. It creates a different quality of work and interaction. That differential compounds over a career into opportunities and relationships that purely professional competence doesn't generate.

I've built a business partly through clients responding to a genuine interest in solving their problems. That engagement attracts people who want to work with someone who cares rather than just completes contracted services.

Look for work that aligns with what you truly care about. Not a dream job necessarily, those are rare. But aspects of work that genuinely interest you that you can emphasize and develop.

Personal life enriches dramatically when shared around interests that matter. Relationships built around shared passions have a different quality than relationships built only around practical coexistence.

Time with my kids around activities we both enjoy creates a connection that managing them through required activities never produces. That shared engagement builds relationships that pure parental obligation doesn't.

Engage family and friends in your interests. Take an interest in theirs. Build relationships around shared passions, not just practical coexistence.

Understand that lifelong passion requires deliberate maintenance. It doesn't just persist automatically. Competing demands and practical concerns constantly pressure you to defer it.

Protect time for what matters. Schedule it. Actually do it. Treat engagement with your interests as essential maintenance, not an optional luxury you'll get to when everything else is handled.

Connect with others who demonstrate that passionate life is possible. Seeing people living this way normalizes it rather than seeming like an unrealistic ideal.

My business mentor network includes people who are passionate about their work and have sustained that engagement for decades. Their example demonstrates it's achievable, not just a theoretical possibility.

Be willing to let specific interests evolve while maintaining a pattern of engagement. What engaged you at twenty-five might not engage you at forty-five. That's normal evolution, not loss of passion.

I've shifted interests multiple times. What matters is maintaining the practice of having interests beyond utility, not preserving specific interests indefinitely.

Remember that lifelong passion isn't constant intensity. It's a sustained connection with what matters through a mix of engaged periods, necessary obligations, difficult challenges, and needed restoration.

That realistic expectation makes it sustainable. Expecting constant enthusiasm burns out. Accepting natural fluctuation while maintaining consistent small engagement sustains connection over decades.

The power of lifelong passion is cumulative. Each year of living this way compounds. Knowledge develops. Capabilities grow. Relationships deepen. Meaning accumulates.

After a decade of building a business I care about, I have developed capabilities, client relationships, and professional satisfaction that I couldn't have achieved through purely mercenary career choices. That accumulated value came from sustained engagement over the years.

What could a decade of sustained passionate engagement build in your life? Where would that accumulated effort lead?

Start now. Small daily engagement compounds remarkably over the years. But only if you actually start and maintain it.

Identify what matters to you now. Not what mattered years ago or what you wish mattered. What actually engages you currently?

Build a small sustainable practice around that. Protect time for it. Connect with others who share it. Let it evolve as you develop.

That simple pattern, maintained over the years, creates a life that feels meaningful rather than just busy. Engaged rather than just obligated. Worth living rather than just enduring.

That's the ultimate power of passion. Not achieving impressive specific outcomes necessarily, though those often follow. But building a daily life that feels genuinely worth living because it's connected to what actually matters to you.

Everything we've covered in this book serves that end. Understanding what passion actually means. Identifying what you care about. Overcoming obstacles. Maintaining motivation. Integrating passion into daily life. Sustaining it over the years.

All of it builds toward a life lived passionately rather than just functionally. That's what makes the effort worthwhile. Not just what you achieve, but how you experience the journey itself.

Start building that life now. Not someday when conditions are perfect. Now, with whatever constraints you're currently facing.

Small sustained engagement with what matters, maintained over years, creates a life that feels fundamentally different from an existence focused only on obligations and practical concerns.

That difference, between life that feels meaningful versus life that feels like just completing required tasks, that's what passion ultimately provides.

Make it your foundation. Build everything else on that. The results will justify the effort many times over.

Epilogue

You've reached the end of this book. But that's not accurate, really.

You've reached the end of reading about passion. The actual work, building life around what matters to you, that's just beginning if you're starting, or continuing if you've already been doing this.

Books create the illusion that knowledge itself changes things. Read about passion, understand principles, feel motivated by examples, that feels like progress. And it is progress of a sort. But it's not the progress that actually matters.

The progress that matters happens when you close this book and apply what resonated with you. Not everything necessarily, trying to implement everything at once becomes overwhelming. But something. One principle. One strategy. One small change aligned with what you actually care about.

I've shared my experience building a business around work I care about while managing MS while raising a family. Not because my path is a blueprint you should copy. Your circumstances differ completely. But because a specific example demonstrates that passionate pursuit is possible despite real constraints, it is not just a theoretical ideal requiring perfect conditions.

Your constraints differ from mine. Your interests and values differ. Your definition of success differs. That's exactly as it should be. The principles apply across different situations. The specific implementation needs to be customized to your reality.

Throughout this book, we've explored passion from multiple angles because it's a complex topic that simplistic advice doesn't adequately address.

What passion actually means beyond vague enthusiasm. How to identify what you genuinely care about versus what you think you should care about. Why understanding your values and authentic self matters for a sustainable, passionate pursuit. The role both psychology and practical strategy play in maintaining engagement over the years.

We've addressed obstacles because they're inevitable and because ignoring them creates a gap between inspiring theory and difficult practice. Fear and self-doubt undermine confidence. Practical constraints that limit options. Social pressure pushing you toward conventional paths. Difficulty of maintaining motivation when progress is slow or setbacks occur.

We've covered strategies for overcoming those obstacles not just through willpower alone, but through systematic approaches that work even when motivation is low. Goal-setting that actually guides action, rather than just creating aspirational statements. Time management that prioritizes what matters, rather than just maximizing busyness. Building support networks that provide real help during difficult periods instead of just feeling good about imagining them.

We've explored how passion integrates into different life domains because compartmentalizing leads to imbalance. Work-life integration that allows professional passion without sacrificing personal relationships. Personal relationships that support rather than compete with professional pursuits. Wellness as a foundation, rather than a luxury, postponed until after success.

We've addressed long-term sustainability because initial enthusiasm is easy, while sustained effort over the years is where most people fail. How to rekindle passion when it fades. How to adapt to changing circumstances without abandoning core commitments. How to measure progress in ways that inform improvement rather than just creating discouragement. How to celebrate milestones that sustain motivation through extended effort.

All of this serves one purpose: helping you build a life where what you actually care about receives consistent investment rather than getting perpetually deferred until someday when conditions are perfect.

That someday never arrives. Conditions are never perfect. If you're waiting for perfect circumstances to pursue what matters, you'll wait indefinitely while life passes by doing things that seem practical but don't fulfill you.

The alternative is starting now. With imperfect knowledge. Amid real constraints. Despite uncertainty about whether you'll succeed. Starting anyway because the cost of not trying, spending life on things that don't matter to you, is higher than the cost of trying and possibly failing.

I didn't know whether I could build a sustainable business after my MS diagnosis. Had serious doubts. Faced real limitations. Made mistakes figuring out what worked. Still make mistakes regularly.

But ten years later, I've built something I'm proud of that provides for my family while being work I genuinely care about. That happened not because I had a perfect plan or ideal circumstances. Because I started despite uncertainty and persisted through difficulty, learning from mistakes and continuously adjusting my approach.

You can do the same. Not necessarily building a consulting business, that's just one possibility among thousands. But building life around what you actually care about rather than just pursuing what seems sensible.

Start small. Pick one thing from this book that resonated. One principle. One strategy. One small practice aligned with what matters to you.

Implement it. Not perfectly, a perfect implementation isn't necessary or realistic. Just implement it as well as you can, given current constraints.

Maintain it for a month. See what happens. Adjust based on experience.

Then add another small practice. Build gradually rather than trying a complete life overhaul immediately.

That incremental approach compounds over months and years into a substantial transformation. Not a dramatic instant change, but accumulated small changes sustained over time.

The power isn't in any single principle or strategy. It's in the consistent application of multiple approaches over an extended period. That sustained effort, guided by genuine care about what you're building, eventually produces results that sporadic, intense effort never achieves.

You have everything you need to start. Knowledge of principles. Awareness of obstacles. Strategies for navigating them. Understanding of how to sustain effort over time.

What you need now isn't more information. It's commitment to application. To actually implement what you've learned rather than just feeling good about understanding it.

Make that commitment. Start today. One small action aligned with what you actually care about.

Then another tomorrow. And the next day. Small, consistent actions compounded over months and years.

That's how passionate life gets built. Not through dramatic transformation, but through accumulated small deliberate choices maintained over time.

Everything in this book supports that building process. Return to relevant chapters when you face specific challenges. Use strategies that fit your situation. Adapt approaches based on your experience.

But most importantly: actually do the building. Knowledge without application is just entertainment. Application, even an imperfect application, creates actual results.

Your life won't look like mine. Shouldn't look like mine. It should look like an authentic expression of your values, interests, and circumstances.

Build that deliberately. Starting now. With what you have. Where you are.

That's what passionate life actually requires. Not perfect conditions. Not complete knowledge. Not absence of fear or doubt.

Just commitment to building around what matters despite imperfect conditions, incomplete knowledge, present fear, and existing constraints.

Start building.

Appendix

Quick Reference: Key Principles

Understanding Passion

- Passion is a sustained interest in an activity or pursuit that aligns with your values.

- It requires both genuine care about outcomes and strategic capability to achieve them.

- It fluctuates naturally; the goal is maintaining engagement through fluctuations, not constant intensity.

Identifying What Matters

- Distinguish between what you think should matter and what actually matters to you.

- Look for activities where you lose track of time and feel energized rather than drained.

- Your values reveal what matters, and examine where you actually invest time and energy.

Overcoming Obstacles

- Fear and self-doubt are normal; progress comes from acting despite them, not eliminating them.

- Practical constraints require adaptation, not abandonment of what matters.

- Setbacks provide information about what to adjust, not verdicts on whether to quit.

Sustaining Effort

- Build systems and routines that maintain engagement regardless of motivation levels.

- Small, consistent actions compound more reliably than sporadic, intense efforts.

- Protect restoration activities; they enable sustained performance, not obstacles to it.

Integration with Life

- Work and personal life aren't separate; integrate passion into both domains.

- Relationships either support passionate pursuits or compete with them; build supportive ones deliberately.

- Health is the foundation for sustained effort, not a luxury postponed until after success.

Practical Tools

Daily Practices

- Morning routine that connects you with what matters before reactive mode begins.

- 15-minute minimum engagement with passionate pursuit regardless of motivation.

- Evening reflection, noting what felt meaningful during the day.

- Weekly review assessing whether activities align with stated priorities.

Goal-Setting Framework

- Annual goals broken into quarterly milestones and monthly targets.

- Concrete next actions for each goal (not just abstract aspirations).

- Regular review comparing intentions to actual results.

- Willingness to adjust goals based on evolved understanding.

Time Management

- Protected time blocks for goal-related work (scheduled like important meetings).

- Batching similar activities to reduce context-switching costs.

- Saying no to low-value demands to create space for what matters.

- Distinguishing between productive pushing and destructive grinding.

Progress Tracking

- Visible tracking showing advancement, not just distance to destination.

- Monthly operational metrics and quarterly strategic assessment.

- Celebration of milestones, providing regular reinforcement.

- Documentation of solved problems, building evidence of capability.

Support Structures

- Accountability partners or groups sharing similar pursuits.

- Mentors who've navigated similar challenges.

- Communities aligned with your interests and values

- Regular check-ins create external pressure when internal motivation dips.

Resources for Continued Learning

Journaling

- Track moments of genuine engagement and energy.

- Note what works and what doesn't in your approaches.

- Reflect on progress and areas needing adjustment.

- Document solved problems as evidence of capability.

Community Connection

- Online forums for people pursuing similar paths.

- Local meetup groups aligned with your interests.

- Professional networks in your field.

- Accountability groups meeting regularly.

Skill Development

- Courses addressing capability gaps.

- Books by people who've done what you're attempting.

- Workshops providing hands-on practice.

- Mentorship for personalized guidance.

Final Reminders

Stay Authentic: Your path won't look like anyone else's. That's not failure, it's individuality. Build around your actual values and interests, not borrowed aspirations.

Be Persistent: Meaningful achievement requires sustained effort over the years. Small, consistent actions compound into significant results that sporadic, intense efforts never produce.

Embrace Adaptation: Circumstances change. You change. Your interests evolve. Adapt approaches while maintaining commitment to core purposes that still matter.

Protect Sustainability: Burnout helps no one. Build a pace you can maintain for years. Intensity that's unsustainable ultimately produces less than sustainable effort.

Celebrate Progress: Acknowledge advancement regularly. Waiting only for major milestones means spending years without reinforcement. Small wins deserve recognition.

Start Now: Perfect conditions never arrive. Start with what you have, where you are, despite imperfect knowledge and present constraints.

The work begins when reading ends. Make it count!